AI L

Questions and Answers

HISTORY

MODERN BRITISH AND EUROPEAN

Michael Scaife   Principal Examiner
Russell Williams   Chief Examiner

SERIES EDITOR: BOB McDUELL

EDUCATIONAL

Key developments

1867	Second Reform Act
1868–74	Gladstone's first ministry
1869	Disestablishment of the Irish Church
1870	First Irish Land Act. Forster's Education Act. Civil service reform
1871	Trade Union Act. Criminal Law Amendment Act
1872	Ballot Act. Licensing Act
1874–80	Disraeli's second ministry
1875	Public Health Act. Artisans' Dwellings Act. Conspiracy and Protection of Property Act. Employers and Workmen Act. Sale of Food and Drugs Act. Merchant Shipping Act. Purchase of Suez Canal shares
1876	Education Act. Queen Victoria made Empress of India
1878	Congress of Berlin. Afghan War
1879	Zulu War
1880–85	Gladstone's second ministry
1881	Second Irish Land Act
1882	Kilmainham Treaty. Phoenix Park murders
1884	Third Reform Act
1886	Gladstone's third ministry. First Home Rule Bill
1892–4	Gladstone's fourth ministry
1893	Second Home Rule Bill

The 1867 Reform Act

The Second Reform Act was mainly the work of Disraeli. It gave the vote to male householders in the boroughs; extended the county franchise; and redistributed seats to larger counties and industrial towns. The main result was to enfranchise the urban working class. Despite the fact that the Act was the work of a Conservative government, the new voters elected Gladstone and the Liberals in 1868.

Gladstone's first ministry, 1868–74

Irish affairs.   Gladstone declared in 1868: 'My mission is to pacify Ireland.' To this end the Irish Church was disestablished in 1869. In 1870 the First Land Act was passed; by this, evicted tenants were to be compensated for improvements, unless evicted for non-payment of rent. The Act failed to stop evictions because there was no effective provision to stop landlords raising rents.

The ministry's **domestic reforms** covered education, trade unions, the secret ballot, licensing of public houses, the civil service, the army and the administration of justice. These reforms were directed primarily towards eliminating privileges rather than improving social conditions. This, along with free trade and strict economy in government finances, was at the heart of 'Gladstonian liberalism'. Many of the reforms alienated different sections of the electorate – a main reason for the defeat of the Liberals in the 1874 election.

Gladstone's **foreign policy** was widely criticised, especially over Russia's repudiation of the Black Sea clauses and the payment of compensation to the USA for the *Alabama*.

Disraeli's second ministry, 1874–80

In **domestic affairs**, reforms were passed concerning public health, working-class housing, picketing by strikers, employees' contracts, food adulteration, education and merchant shipping. Most of these Acts were the work of the Home Secretary, Cross. They form the evidence for an analysis of the practical meaning of 'Tory democracy'. The weakness was that many of the Acts were permissive (e.g. the Artisans Dwellings' Act).

In **foreign affairs**, the ministry was dominated by the **Balkan crisis of 1875–8**. Turkish brutality in suppressing a revolt in the Balkans (the Bulgarian atrocities) made it difficult to support Turkey and provoked a savage denunciation by Gladstone. But when Russia intervened and threatened Constantinople, the traditional British fear of Russian expansion into the Mediterranean was aroused and Disraeli sent a fleet to Constantinople. Russia then made peace with Turkey (the Treaty of San Stefano); this set up a 'big' Bulgaria, which Disraeli feared would be under Russian control. Working with Bismarck, he put pressure on Russia to agree to the **Congress of Berlin**, as a result of which Bulgaria was reduced in size and Britain gained Cyprus. The Congress was regarded as a triumph for Disraeli.

Disraeli was also very active in **imperial affairs**. His policies were popular at first. In 1875 he purchased the Suez Canal shares and in 1876 he created the title Empress of India for Queen Victoria. But in 1878–9 his 'forward' policies led to the outbreak of the Afghan and Zulu Wars, in both of which British troops suffered defeats before they were eventually successful. Public opinion began to see Disraeli's imperialism as dangerous, and this contributed to his defeat in 1880.

Gladstone's second ministry, 1880–85

In **Ireland**, Gladstone brought in the Second Land Act which gave Irish tenants the three Fs. However, the Irish situation had changed greatly since 1870:

(a) The Irish Land League had organised a militant campaign of rent strikes, boycotts and agrarian outrages.

(b) Parnell had emerged at the head of a Home Rule Party.

To maintain order in Ireland, Gladstone had to introduce a new Coercion Act (1881), as a result of which Parnell was arrested. In 1882, in an attempt to restore peace in Ireland, Gladstone made the Kilmainham Treaty with Parnell, but this was immediately followed by the Phoenix Park murders. The murders helped to convince Gladstone that Home Rule was the only answer – but they also turned English opinion *against* the Irish.

In **imperial affairs**, Gladstone's two main problems were the legacy of Disraeli:

(a) In **South Africa**, the Zulus were defeated, but this led to problems with Transvaal, which, freed from the Zulu threat, declared itself independent. The First Boer War resulted in a British defeat at Majuba Hill and the recognition of Transvaal's virtual independence.

(b) Britain became involved in the internal affairs of **Egypt**, where in 1882 British forces took control. Further trouble arose in Sudan, where General Gordon was cut off in Khartoum and killed along with his force. This brought Gladstone much unpopularity.

In **domestic affairs**, the most important reform was the Third Reform Act (1884), which gave the vote to agricultural labourers. The failure of this ministry to tackle social reform led to increasing tension between Gladstone and Joseph Chamberlain.

Gladstone and Irish Home Rule

The 1885 general election gave Parnell's Irish Home Rule Party the balance of power. Gladstone's son then revealed his father's conversion to Home Rule. With Irish support, Gladstone formed his third ministry in 1886 and introduced a Home Rule Bill. This split the Liberal Party: 93 Liberals, led by Joseph Chamberlain and Hartington, voted against it and it was defeated in the Commons. The split in the Liberal Party ushered in 20 years of largely Conservative government, during which the Liberal Unionists (those Liberals who had voted against Home Rule) moved over to become allies of the Conservatives.

In 1892 Gladstone, with Irish support, formed his fourth ministry. The Second Home Rule Bill (1893) passed the Commons but was defeated in the Lords. Gladstone then retired.

If you need to revise this subject more thoroughly, see the relevant topic in the *Letts* A-level *British History Study Guide*.

1   'It was Irish extremism rather than British timidity that doomed every effort to solve the Irish problem.' Discuss with reference to 1868–94.   (30)

Oxford & Cambridge

2   Were there significant differences of principle dividing Gladstone and Disraeli or were they simply rivals for power?   (25)

NICCEA

3   Consider the view that 'Gladstone was more of a liability than an asset to the Liberal Party in the period 1865–1894'.   (25)

AEB

4   How and why did Gladstone lose the support of Joseph Chamberlain?   (25)

Oxford

5   To what extent were Disraeli's policies between 1866 and 1880 guided by the spirit of 'Tory democracy'?   (25)

Cambridge

4 The Edwardian age, 1901–14

Key developments

1895–1905	Conservative ministries of Salisbury and Balfour
1900	Formation of Labour Representation Committee
1901	Taff Vale judgement
1905–14	Liberal ministries of Campbell-Bannerman and Asquith
1906	General election: overwhelming Liberal victory
1909	Lloyd George's 'People's Budget'
1910	Two general elections
1911	Parliament Act. National Insurance Act
1912–14	Third Home Rule Bill

The 1906 election

In the **election of 1906** the Conservatives were heavily defeated. Probably the main reason was that they were split because of the **tariff reform** campaign which Chamberlain began in 1903. Another reason was that in the light of the work of Booth and Rowntree, there was a growing demand for social reform, which the Conservatives had failed to meet. The 1902 Education Act, the Taff Vale case and the Chinese labour scandal were also factors.

The Liberal governments, 1905–14

The Liberal ministries were notable for their **social reforms**:

- Children: school meals for needy children; medical inspection in schools; the Children's Charter.

- Old people: pensions – 5 shillings a week at 70, provided other income below £26 per annum.

- Workers in certain industries: the Trade Boards Act; the Shops Act; the Mines Act.

- The unemployed: employment exchanges were set up.

- National Insurance Act, 1911, providing insurance against sickness ('9 pence for 4 pence') and against unemployment (only for workers in certain industries).

These measures are sometimes regarded as the origin of the welfare state.

There were also two Acts concerning trade unions: the Trade Disputes Act (1906), which reversed the Taff Vale judgement, and the Trade Union Act (1913), which reversed the Osborne judgement.

The 1909 budget and the struggle with the Lords

Lloyd George's budget of 1909 proposed radical tax changes including a tax on land values, which was particularly objectionable to the House of Lords, most of whose members were landowners. The Lords had already obstructed other Liberal Bills. Lloyd George may have made his budget proposals with the deliberate intention of provoking a quarrel with the Lords. The Lords rejected the budget, which was unprecedented and raised the question of the power of the hereditary house to overrule the elected house. After two general elections in 1910, both of which returned the Liberals to power with the support of the Labour and Irish MPs, the Lords were forced to accept both the budget and the **Parliament Act**, which had three main provisions: (a) the Lords were no longer able to reject a money Bill; (b) their power to reject other Bills was reduced to a two-year delaying power; (c) the interval between general elections was reduced to five years. At the same time payment of MPs (£400 p.a.) was started.

Ireland

The Irish Nationalists supported the Parliament Act in the expectation that their reward would be Home Rule. Under the provisions of the Parliament Act, a Home Rule Bill introduced in 1912 became law in 1914 despite the opposition of the Lords. The Ulster Protestants, however, refused to accept Home Rule and, under the leadership of Carson, armed themselves in preparation for civil war. The nationalists in the south responded with similar preparations.

Furthermore, the Curragh Mutiny showed that the government could not rely on the army to enforce Home Rule. The outbreak of the First World War enabled the government to escape from the problem for the time being by suspending the Act.

Suffragettes

The period of Liberal rule was also marked by the growing militancy of the **suffragettes**. Majority opinion in the government was opposed to giving women the vote and militancy only hardened their opposition. Hunger strikes were countered by the Cat and Mouse Act. It was largely the role of women during the war which finally won them the vote in 1918.

Rise of the Labour Party

In the mid-nineteenth century **trade unions** developed among skilled workers. These unions were not politically orientated, although from the 1870s there were a few Liberal MPs with a working-class background. In the 1880s, trade unions began to spread among unskilled workers, a trend which was greatly boosted by the success of the London dockers' strike of 1889. These 'new unions' were more prone to take strike action and more interested in using political means to improve working-class conditions. During the 1870s and 1880s a number of **socialist societies** emerged, notably the Social Democratic Federation and the Fabian Society. Keir Hardie, the Scottish miners' leader, who was MP for West Ham from 1892 to 1895, took the lead in setting up the Independent Labour Party in 1893.

In 1900 the **Labour Representation Committee** was set up: this drew together the trade unions and the socialist societies with the aim of securing the election of 'Labour' MPs. In 1906, 29 Labour MPs were elected as well as 24 Lib-Labs. In the same year the name 'Labour Party' was adopted. In December 1910 the Labour Party won 42 seats.

REVISION SUMMARY

If you need to revise this subject more thoroughly, see the relevant topic in the *Letts* A-level *British History Study Guide*.

QUESTIONS

1 To what extent did political advantage account for the interest shown by both Conservatives and Liberals in social and economic reform in the period 1900–14?   (25)

WJEC

2 Read the following extract about the beginning of the Labour Party from *The Rise of the Labour Party, 1880–1945* by Paul Adelman, and then answer the questions which follow.

'… a small committee representing the trade unions and the socialist societies met together and arranged for the summoning of a conference to discuss the problems of organising increased labour representation. This met in London on 27 February 1900, at the Memorial Hall in Farringdon Street, and it is this meeting that has been looked upon as marking the foundation of the Labour Party.'

(a) Explain what had been the main 'problems of organising increased labour representation' in the years before 1900.   (4)

(b) To what extent did the aims of the new Labour Party reflect its desire to bring about social change?   (6)

(c) How successful both in influencing the policies of the two major Parties and in gaining support for its own was the new Party in the years from 1900 to 1906?   (10)

NEAB

3 'A victory which owed more to Tory divisions and mistakes than it did to any Liberal programme of reform': discuss this view of the result of the 1906 General Election.   (25)

ULEAC

4 'A serious quarrel between political parties, but not a constitutional crisis': discuss this opinion of the 'Parliamentary crisis' of 1909 to 1911.   (25)

ULEAC

5 Britain, Europe and the Empire, 1885–1914

REVISION SUMMARY

Key developments

1885	Berlin Treaty defines 'spheres of influence' in Africa
1887	Mediterranean agreements
1890	Treaties with Germany, Portugal and France over partition of Africa
1891	Dual alliance of France and Russia completes Britain's isolation
1895	Jameson Raid
1898	Fashoda Incident. German Naval Law
1899–1902	Second Boer War
1902	Anglo–Japanese Alliance
1904	Entente Cordiale
1905	First Morocco Crisis
1906	Algeciras Conference. *Dreadnought* launched
1907	Anglo-Russian Entente
1911	Agadir Crisis
1912	Anglo-French Naval Agreement
1914	German invasion of Belgium. Britain declares war on Germany

'Splendid isolation'

In the late nineteenth century the great powers divided into the Triple Alliance and the Dual Alliance (see Unit 10). Britain joined neither. It regarded maintaining and strengthening links with the overseas Empire as its overriding interest. Naval superiority was the guarantee both of this and of its own security. Britain was therefore unwilling to be drawn into unnecessary commitments to continental allies.

Chamberlain and imperialism

The late nineteenth century also witnessed further expansion of the Empire, particularly in Africa, where Britain became involved in the 'scramble for Africa'. Joseph Chamberlain (Colonial Secretary, 1895–1903), saw the Empire as the solution to Britain's economic problems, in the face of the growing challenge from the USA and Germany. His period at the Colonial Office was marked by the conquest of Sudan, which nearly led to war with France in the Fashoda Incident (1898), and the Second Boer War. Chamberlain's imperialism was also linked to his tariff reform campaign. He envisaged a system of imperial preference as well as protective duties on imports into Britain.

The other key figure in British imperialism in the late nineteenth century was **Rhodes**, who envisaged British colonies from southern Africa to Egypt (the Cape to Cairo Railway). In 1885 he set up a British protectorate over Bechuanaland and in 1889 formed the British South Africa Company to develop colonies in Rhodesia (modern Zimbabwe and Zambia). As a result, the Boer republics of Transvaal and Orange Free State were almost encircled.

The Second Boer War, 1899–1902

The Boer republics had their origin in the desire of the Boers to escape from British rule (the Great Trek, 1835–7). There had already been one war between the British and the Boers in 1880–81. The expansionist policies of Rhodes aroused deep suspicion among the Boers and there were other factors which heightened the tension:

(a) Boer treatment of the 'Uitlanders', the foreigners (mainly British) who went to Transvaal after the discovery of gold in 1886.

(b) The Jameson Raid (1895), in which Rhodes was implicated.

(c) The breakdown of talks between Milner and Kruger on the Uitlander question.

In the war itself, after initial setbacks, the British gained military superiority by 1900 but it took two more years to wear down Boer resistance.

Relations with Germany in the 1890s

In the early 1890s Anglo-German relations were good. Britain was suspicious of French ambitions in Africa and Russian ambitions in Asia. It therefore seemed likely that, if Britain abandoned splendid isolation, it would join the Triple Alliance. However, relations with Germany deteriorated from 1896 because of:

(a) the Kruger telegram, in which William II congratulated Kruger on repelling the Jameson Raid

(b) the German naval laws of 1898 and 1900

(c) pro-Boer attitudes in Germany during the Boer War.

The Ententes

By 1900 increasing friction with Germany, Britain's lack of friends during the Boer War and the realisation that the Fashoda Incident had nearly caused a war with France all highlighted the dangers of 'splendid isolation'. Britain began to seek allies. In 1902 it secured an ally in **Japan**, which provided a safeguard against Russian expansion in the Far East. In Europe, Britain sought an agreement with Germany, but was rebuffed in 1898–9. It turned to France and in 1904 signed the **Entente Cordiale**: France recognised British control in Egypt, while Britain accepted France's ambitions in Morocco. This was followed by an entente with Russia in 1907, in which differences over Persia, Afghanistan and Tibet were resolved. The Triple Entente aligned Britain with France and Russia against the Triple Alliance, but it involved no commitment to go to war. In that sense Britain was not an *ally* of France and Russia, though from 1904 military and naval conversations drew Britain and France closer together.

Britain and the First World War

The crises which led up to the outbreak of war are set out in Unit 10. In explaining how Britain was drawn in, the key issues are imperial rivalry (the two Moroccan crises of 1905 and 1911); the naval race (note the rivalry over *Dreadnoughts* and the Anglo-French Naval Agreement of 1912); and the German invasion of Belgium.

The most important questions to consider are how far, when and why Britain became committed to the support of France and Russia. Would Britain have entered the war if Germany had not invaded Belgium?

1 How far do you agree that Britain, in the first decade of the twentieth century, drifted into foreign commitments that were, in 1914, to involve it in an unnecessary war? (25)
ULEAC

2 'A combination of exaggerated hope and over-heated anxiety.' How adequate is this interpretation of the reasons for British Imperial expansion in the period c.1880–1902? (25)
AEB

3 'In spite of the Boer attacks on Cape Colony in October 1899, the major responsibility for the Second Boer War lay with Britain.' How far do you agree with this view? (25)
Cambridge

4 How far was Britain's retreat from a foreign policy of 'splendid isolation' in the years before 1906 a direct result of the growing threat from Germany? (20)
NEAB

Key developments

	Changes of government	Other developments
1918	Lloyd George (Coalition)	
1921		Black Friday. Irish Treaty
1922	Bonar Law (Conservative)	
1923	Baldwin's first ministry	
1924	MacDonald (Labour)	Zinoviev Letter
	Baldwin's second ministry	
1926		General Strike
1929	MacDonald (Labour)	
1931	MacDonald (National)	Sterling crisis. Gold standard abandoned
1932		Protection introduced
1935	Baldwin (National)	German rearmament, Stresa Front, Anglo-German Naval Treaty. Mussolini's invasion of Abyssinia
1936		Occupation of Rhineland. Abdication crisis
1937	Chamberlain (National)	
1938		Munich
1939		Outbreak of Second World War

Lloyd George's Coalition government, 1918–22

In **foreign affairs**, Lloyd George played a major role in the Versailles Conference. In **domestic affairs**, an attempt was made to honour the promise that post-war Britain would be 'a land fit for heroes to live in' by Addison's housing drive and the Unemployment Insurance Act of 1920. After a brief post-war economic boom, unemployment rose to nearly 2 million in 1922. As a result, public expenditure rose and cuts were made (the Geddes Axe, 1922). There were serious industrial problems, culminating in a miners' strike in 1921; the miners were defeated after the collapse of the Triple Alliance (Black Friday).

Perhaps the most serious domestic problem was **Ireland**. The Easter Rising (1916) had strengthened support for Sinn Fein, which triumphed in Ireland in the 1918 general election and set up an (illegal) Irish parliament in Dublin. A rebellion broke out, which the government tried to suppress with the 'black and tans'. Finally, a 'treaty' was made with Sinn Fein in 1921, as a result of which most of Ireland was given dominion status, but the six counties of Northern Ireland remained part of the United Kingdom, with a parliament for local affairs. This solution came into effect with the establishment of the Irish Free State in 1922, although there was then a civil war in Ireland itself.

In 1922 Lloyd George was overthrown when the Conservatives decided to withdraw from the Coalition (Carlton Club meeting). They had become increasingly unhappy with Lloyd George, who was a Liberal at the head of a mainly Conservative Coalition. The Irish treaty and the **Chanak crisis** were the last straws.

The Conservatives in the 1920s

Baldwin, who played a prominent part in the Carlton Club meeting, became Prime Minister in 1923. Later that year he announced his intention to introduce protection. He called a general election on this issue, and lost, but returned to office after the election of 1924.

In **Baldwin's second ministry (1924–9)**, although overall economic activity grew, unemployment remained high, particularly in the export industries. This was partly because of the decision to return to the gold standard at the pre-war parity (1925). There was a gradual development of state-provided welfare: in 1925 the old age pension scheme was enlarged and the 1929 Local Government Act transferred the functions of the poor law guardians to local authorities. The BBC became a public corporation (1926) and the vote was extended to women aged between 21 and 30 (1928).

The unspectacular nature of much of the work of the ministry was in sharp contrast to the most dramatic event of the 1920s: the **General Strike of 1926**. The strike had its origins in the

problems of the coal industry. The coal owners proposed a wage cut, which the mine workers rejected. A strike was averted by a government subsidy to the industry while awaiting the report of the *Samuel Commission*. When the commission reported both sides rejected its proposals. A miners' strike followed and the miners turned to the TUC for support. Mindful of the collapse of the Triple Alliance in 1921, the TUC ordered a general strike. The government was well prepared and the TUC was half-hearted, so the strike was called off after nine days. The miners were eventually defeated. The government then made general or sympathetic strikes illegal in the **Trade Disputes Act (1927)**.

The two Labour ministries

The first Labour ministry, 1924
In the 1922 election Labour gained more seats than the Liberals and became the official opposition. In the 1923 election, it made further gains. The Conservatives lost their overall majority and MacDonald, as leader of the next largest party, was asked to form a minority government. The main achievements of the first Labour ministry were the Wheatley Housing Act; increased unemployment benefits; and the restoration of diplomatic relations with the USSR. MacDonald also played an important role in negotiating the Dawes Plan and the Geneva Protocol. However, the ministry depended on Liberal support, which it lost over the Campbell case. The subsequent general election was heavily influenced by the Zinoviev letter and the Conservatives won a big majority.

The second Labour ministry (1929–31)
This was formed as a result of the election of 1929, in which Labour emerged for the first time as the biggest party, though still without an overall majority and therefore dependent on the Liberals. It achieved little before it was overtaken by economic crisis resulting from the Great Depression. By 1931 unemployment had risen to 2.75 million. As a result, expenditure on benefits went up, while the tax yield went down. The May Committee, appointed to find ways of balancing the budget, produced an alarming report in July 1931, which led to a run on the pound. The Chancellor of the Exchequer, Snowden, wanted to cut unemployment benefit to save the pound, as proposed by the May Committee, but the Cabinet could not agree on this and the Labour government resigned.

The rise of Labour in the 1920s was accompanied by a rapid decline of the Liberal Party.

The National governments, 1931–9
When the second Labour ministry collapsed in 1931, MacDonald became Prime Minister of a National government, supported by the Conservatives and most of the Liberals. Only a handful of Labour MPs followed MacDonald. In the 1931 general election the National government won an overwhelming victory; Labour was reduced to 52 seats. The National governments were Conservative-dominated even though they had a Labour Prime Minister from 1931 to 1935. Baldwin was effectively the joint leader of the government. In 1935 he became Prime Minister and was succeeded in 1937 by Chamberlain.

Economic policies of the National governments
The immediate financial crisis was tackled by 10 per cent cuts in public sector pay and unemployment benefit, and the highly unpopular Means Test was introduced. The government was nevertheless forced to abandon the gold standard in 1931. Although great efforts had been made to avoid this, it actually benefited British exports. In 1932 protective tariffs were introduced, along with a scheme of imperial preference set up at the Ottawa Conference. The unemployment benefit system was reorganised by the creation in 1935 of the Unemployment Assistance Board. An attempt was made to tackle the problem of the decline of the older industrial areas by the Special Areas Act (1934). Marketing boards were set up for agricultural products such as milk.

By 1933 economic recovery was under way, though this was more due to a housing boom and the revival of world trade than to government policies. By 1937 unemployment had fallen to

REVISION
SUMMARY

just over 1 million, though much of this was concentrated in the older industrial areas, where it remained a serious problem and a source of much bitterness.

Foreign Policy

The National governments responded to the aggressive nationalism of Japan, Italy and Germany by pursuing a policy of **appeasement**.

Japan. Although the Lytton Commission, appointed by the League of Nations, condemned Japan for invading Manchuria, Britain was unwilling to take any action.

Italy. When Italy invaded Abyssinia, Britain supported the imposition of sanctions by the League but opposed the inclusion of oil. Britain was reluctant to alienate Italy, whose support was needed in opposing German rearmament (Stresa Front, 1935). The Foreign Secretary, Hoare, was so keen to keep Italy's friendship that he proposed in the *Hoare-Laval Pact* to allow Italy to control most of Abyssinia. Public opinion would not stomach this and Hoare was forced to resign. Nevertheless Italy got away with its aggression.

Germany. Britain protested against German rearmament (1935), joining the Stresa Front with France and Italy. Later in 1935, however, in the Anglo-German Naval Agreement, it accepted German naval rearmament. In 1936 Britain made little protest about Hitler's reoccupation of the Rhineland. In 1938 it accepted the *Anschluss* on the grounds that Austria was German in nationality. Later in 1938, when Hitler demanded the Sudetenland, Chamberlain flew to Germany three times to negotiate with him, and finally gave way to all of his demands at Munich. Chamberlain was unwilling to risk war on behalf of a 'far away' country and believed Hitler's statement that this was his last territorial claim in Europe.

War, 1939

Chamberlain's policy changed in 1939 when Hitler took over the rest of Czechoslovakia. When Hitler invaded Poland in September 1939, Britain declared war.

If you need to revise this subject more thoroughly, see the relevant topic in the *Letts* A-level *British History Study Guide*.

QUESTIONS

1 Explain the dominance of the Conservative Party in British politics in the inter-war period. (25)
NICCEA

2 'Appeasement before 1936 was a sensible and practical policy for Britain; after 1936 it was not.' How far do you agree with this view? (25)
Cambridge

3 Read the following extract about the General Strike of 1926 from *Empire to Welfare State: English History, 1906–1976* by T. O. Lloyd, and then answer the questions which follow.

'The miners' stand was not flexible: "Not a minute on the day, not a penny off the pay". Nor were the owners more helpful: district agreements, longer hours and lower wages was their answer.'

(a) How far was the General Strike caused by lack of flexibility on the part of both mine workers and mine owners? (12)

(b) Why did the General Strike fail? (8)
NEAB

4 'A successful administration with a creditable record of reform.' Discuss this verdict on Stanley Baldwin's government of 1924–9. (25)
WJEC

5 'Ramsay MacDonald betrayed his party in 1931 and undid all that he had achieved for Labour since 1918.' How far do you agree? (25)
Oxford

6 How successfully did governments tackle Britain's economic problems between the two world wars? (30)
Oxford & Cambridge

International diplomacy, 1815–56 7

Key developments

1814	Abdication of Napoleon. Congress of Vienna
1815	Waterloo. Vienna settlement. Quadruple Alliance. Holy Alliance
1818	Congress of Aix-la-Chapelle
1820	Revolutions in Spain, Naples, Portugal. Congress of Troppau
1821	Revolt in Greece. Congress of Laibach
1822	Congress of Verona
1829	Treaty of Adrianople
1830	Greek independence
1831–9	Belgian independence
1841	Straits Convention
1854–6	Crimean War
1856	Peace of Paris

The Vienna settlement

Belgium, Holland and Luxemburg were united in the kingdom of the Netherlands.
Lombardy-Venetia was controlled by Austria. **The German Confederation** of 39 states was
established under the presidency of Austria. **Prussia** received Posen, Danzig and parts of
Saxony, Westphalia and Pomerania. **Britain** gained overseas territories, Malta, Heligoland and
the Cape of Good Hope. **The Pope** regained the Papal States. **Norway** was united with **Sweden**.
Russia gained **Finland**. **Switzerland** became independent.

Legitimate rulers were restored in France, Spain, Naples, Tuscany and other parts of Italy.
Free navigation was established on the rivers Rhine and Meuse. The slave trade was condemned.
The rights of Jews were extended.

Why the settlement?
Austria (Metternich), **Britain** (Castlereagh and Wellington), **Prussia** (Hardenberg) and **Russia**
(Alexander I) were determined to settle Europe after the years of the French Revolution and the
Napoleonic Wars. Talleyrand was admitted to represent **France**.

The settlement was a series of **compromises**. France was contained but not harshly punished.
Russian expansion in eastern Europe was feared and limited. Austria gained influence in
Germany and Italy. Prussia extended its territories. Britain's main interests were overseas. Minor
states were treated as pawns. Some were combined to form larger states. Former rulers were
restored. But nationalist feeling was thought unimportant, even dangerous, by the major powers.

The Vienna settlement has been seen by some historians as a **sensible arrangement**. It was
the best that could be expected in 1815 after the Napoleonic Wars, preventing war until 1854.
Others have seen Vienna as showing the **self-interest** of the major states. Some of the terms
were soon to cause trouble, especially as nationalism spread through Europe and people sought
independence, e.g. in Italy, Germany and Belgium.

The Congress System

The Congress System was an attempt to maintain peace and order through the combined
influence and actions of the major states. Some historians believe that the term 'System' is
inaccurate because there was nothing systematic about the meetings and that they were
individual responses to crises. Others see the congresses as a significant attempt to resolve
tensions.

Austria, Britain, Prussia and Russia formed the **Quadruple Alliance** and agreed to
maintain peace (**the Concert of Europe**). But the major powers had different aims. **Austria** and
Russia favoured intervention against revolutions; **Britain** did not wish to intervene in internal
disputes.

Congresses were held to resolve disputes. At **Aix-la-Chapelle**, France was admitted to the Quintuple Alliance; the occupation of France ended. **Troppau** was a response to revolts in Spain, Portugal, Piedmont and Naples. Britain opposed intervention. At **Laibach**, Austria and Russia were ready to send soldiers against Italian revolts. Britain again opposed intervention. The Greek revolt caused disagreements. Britain (represented by Canning) withdrew at **Verona** when French troops were used against rebellion in Spain. Only Austria, Prussia and Russia met at **St Petersburg** (1825), an unsuccessful attempt to resolve their problems.

Revolutionary movements

Soon after 1815, nationalist movements developed to threaten stability. Metternich was particularly concerned to stabilise the **Austrian empire** with its many races. The **German Diet**, encouraged by Metternich, passed the Carlsbad Decrees (1819) to suppress liberal groups. There were more reactionary measures in the 1830s. In **Italy**, the Risorgimento ('Resurrection') movement developed. Following the failure of the 1830 revolution to unite Italy, Mazzini founded the 'Young Italy' movement (1831). **Belgium** became independent (1831) and its neutrality was confirmed (1839). **Poland** rebelled against Russia (1830 and 1846). **Greece** won its independence from the Turkish empire in 1830. A revolution against the absolute policies of Charles X of **France** resulted in his abdication and the monarchy of Louis Philippe.

The Eastern Question

The **Eastern Question** was a particularly tangled problem in which the interests of all of the major European powers and the Turkish empire were concerned. It began well before the nineteenth century and continued well into the twentieth century. There is a direct link between the Eastern Question and the troubles in the Balkans which were to cause the First World War.

A declining **Turkish empire** ('the sick man of Europe') controlled much of the Balkans and Middle East. **Russia** wished to gain direct access to the Mediterranean through the Dardanelles and to protect the rights of Orthodox Christians in the Muslim Turkish empire. **Austria** had its own empire in the Balkans and did not favour the growth of Russian power. **Britain** feared Russian expansion into the Mediterranean and Middle East because of its own interests in the region and in the route to India. **France** wished to secure the rights to protect Christian holy places in Palestine.

After 1815, British and French suspicions of Russia increased. Successive treaties, e.g. the Treaty of Unkiar Skelessi (1833) and the Straits Convention (1841), did not resolve the problem. The **Crimean War** broke out in 1854 with Britain, France and later Piedmont joining the Ottoman empire against Russia. Although Austria opposed Russia, it did not intervene.

In the **Peace of Paris** (1856) Russia surrendered its claims to land and the protectorate of Orthodox Christians, Turkey allowed disputed regions some self-government and the Black Sea was closed to all warships, most importantly Russia's.

It was an unsuccessful attempt to resolve the Eastern Question. Turkey continued to decline. Russia maintained its ambitions in the region and the peoples of the Balkans sought independence from Turkey. Britain continued to suspect Russian motives.

The Crimean War also had important internal effects on countries. Alexander II, the new tsar of Russia, became convinced of the need for reform. Austria was isolated. Napoleon III of France was encouraged to pursue a bold foreign policy. Piedmont had taken a small, but important, step to the leadership of Italy.

If you need to revise this subject more thoroughly, see the relevant topic in the *Letts* A-level European History Study Guide.

1 'A cynical exercise in national self-interest.' 'A considered attempt to restore the European balance of power.' Which of these two statements offers the more accurate view of the Congress of Vienna of 1814–15? Refer to both statements in your answer. (20)

NEAB

2 To what extent does Metternich deserve the reputation of being the most important European statesman in the period 1815–1848? (25)

Oxford

3 How far was the Vienna Settlement more threatened by the events of 1848–1849 than by the revolutions of 1830? (25)

AEB

4 What was the Congress System? Why had it come to an end by 1827? (15)

ULEAC

5 Why, and with what consequences for international stability, were other major European powers suspicious of Russia's intentions towards the Ottoman empire during the years 1825 to 1856? (25)

Cambridge

6 (a) Write a sentence to explain why Turkey was described in the 1850s as 'the sick man of Europe'. (2)

(b) Write a sentence to explain ONE reason for Russia's interests in the Balkans at this time. (2)

(c) Write one or two sentences to explain how the other European nations reacted to Russia's interest in the Balkans. (3)

(d) Write one or two sentences to explain how the Straits Convention limited Russia's ambitions in the Balkans. (3)

(e) Write a paragraph to explain the immediate causes of the Crimean War. (5)

ULEAC

8 *Nationalism and unification: Italy and Germany*

Key developments

	Italy	Germany
1815	Vienna: Italy under Austrian influence	Vienna: Confederation of 39 states under Austrian influence
1831	Mazzini founded Young Italy	
1833		Zollverein; German free-trade area, excluding Austria
1848	Revolutions: crushed by Austria	Revolutions: crushed by Austria and Prussia
1852	Cavour Prime Minister of Piedmont	
1860	Union of Piedmont with northern states	
1861	Proclamation of Kingdom of Italy. Death of Cavour	
1862		Bismarck Chief Minister of Prussia
1866		Seven Weeks' War against Austria.
1867		North German Confederation
1870	Incorporation of Rome into Italy	Franco-Prussian War
1871		Proclamation of German empire at Versailles

The growth of nationalism – Italy

- **Mazzini**, founder of '**Young Italy**', wished to make Italy '**independent, united, free**', and he believed that Austria could be defeated by Italy's efforts alone. The 1848 revolution failed. Nevertheless, his influence lasted through the memory of 1848 and through his followers, such as **Garibaldi**. Although his ideas of a united Italy were different from those of the monarchist and Piedmontese Cavour, he helped to shape the pattern of the Italy of 1870.

- **Gioberti** supported a confederation, not a union, of Italian states. He was defeated in 1848–9 and his views were rejected by later nationalists.

- **Pius IX** became Pope in 1846 with the reputation of being a liberal, but the outbreak of revolution in 1848 alarmed him. He opposed Cavour's policies and, when Rome was incorporated into Italy in 1870, he refused to recognise the new state.

- **Charles Albert**, king of Piedmont, introduced economic reforms. His aim was to create a larger kingdom of north Italy rather than unite all of the peninsula. He believed that Italy could free itself ('*Farà da sè*'), but abdicated (1849) after defeat by the Austrian army at Custozza.

- **Garibaldi** was a republican member of Mazzini's 'Young Italy'. In 1848–9 he joined the revolutionaries in Italy, before returning to exile after the failure of the revolutions. In 1859 he invaded Sicily and Naples with the 'Thousand Red-Shirts' and he was important in persuading Cavour to include the south in the new Italy.

Achievement of unification

Cavour, Prime Minister of Piedmont from 1852, aimed to modernise Piedmont and to create a **kingdom of northern Italy** under Piedmont's leadership. He did not favour the inclusion of the southern states in a new Italy because they were economically backward and politically unstable.

He was an **opportunist** who took advantage of the Crimean War to gain the sympathy of Napoleon III of France. At Plombières (1858) Napoleon III agreed on a joint war against Austria. His withdrawal after initial victories caused Cavour to resign but he soon returned to office.

Cavour also used **plebiscites** to gain support for Piedmont's expansion in Parma, Modena, Tuscany and the Romagna (1860). He tried to obstruct Garibaldi's campaign to capture Sicily and Naples but popular opinion forced him to accept the southern states as part of the unified state. The Kingdom of Italy was proclaimed in 1861. Venetia and Rome were still excluded. Italy gained Venetia (1866) as a by-product of the Austro-Prussian War. French soldiers ended their protection of Rome because of the Franco-Prussian War (1870). Rome was then incorporated in Italy.

The growth of nationalism – Germany

Although they were governed by authoritarian rulers, many states, such as Prussia, had constitutions which gave rights to citizens. There were strong regional differences, including language and religion. Unlike Italy, Germany had an institution (the **Bundestag**) in which the different states were represented.

The first important step towards unity was economic. The **Zollverein** (1833), an agreement to abolish tariffs between states, included almost all German states but – crucially – excluded Austria. Prussia's growing economy helped to increase its influence.

The 1848 revolutions

The most important development was the meeting of the **Frankfurt Parliament**. Elected on a wide male suffrage throughout Germany, its members were largely middle class. They agreed a constitution but Frederick William IV refused the crown of a united Germany.

The members disagreed about the extent of 'Germany' – a 'Little Germany' ('*Kleindeutsch*') without Austria or a 'Great Germany' ('*Grossdeutsch*'), which might be dominated by Austria. The parliament broke up in confusion and Prussia helped to restore order after a few minor risings.

Achievement of unification

Bismarck opposed the liberal revolution of 1848. He was appointed Chief Minister of Prussia (1862) because of a budget crisis with the liberals. **Historians debate Bismarck's attitude to a united Germany**. Some believe that unity was always his long-term goal but the majority see him as an opportunist who was preoccupied with extending Prussian power and weakening Austria, taking advantage of events which he could not foresee.

To prepare for the struggle with Austria, Bismarck sought the friendship of Russia, France and the new state of Italy. Russia remained neutral after Bismarck had given support during a revolt in Poland. Napoleon III of France was bought off by some vague promises of territorial concessions. Britain was unwilling to intervene.

Unification was achieved in three stages:

❶ **1864: Schleswig-Holstein**. Prussia and Austria defeated Denmark. Prussia gained Schleswig.

❷ **1866: The Seven Weeks' War**. Prussia defeated Austria at Sadowa. The Peace of Prague excluded Austria from Germany. The North German Confederation, dominated by Prussia and largely Protestant, was established.

❸ **1870: The Franco-Prussian War**. Napoleon III was defeated at Sedan and France conceded Alsace-Lorraine, paying a large indemnity. The south German states, largely Catholic, joined the Confederation to form the German empire (1871). William I became Emperor (or Kaiser) and Bismarck was Chancellor.

If you need to revise this subject more thoroughly, see the relevant topic in the *Letts* A-level *European History Study Guide*.

QUESTIONS

1   How far was Cavour the architect of Italian unification? (25)
Oxford

2   (a) Identify four German states which existed prior to unification. (4)

   (b) Explain the significance of the Schleswig-Holstein Question in Austro-Prussian relations. (5)

   (c) To what extent had Bismarck been able to bring about the diplomatic isolation of Austria by 1867? (7)

   (d) Did the Seven Weeks' War finally resolve the causes of Austro-Prussian rivalry? Explain your answer fully. (9)
WJEC

3   Why did Piedmont become the effective focus of the movement for Italian unification? (25)
Cambridge

4   Consider the view that 'the continuation of social, political and religious divisions in Italy in the period 1861–1870 demonstrates that Italian Unification was the accidental achievement of a vocal minority'. (25)
AEB

5   'Garibaldi's only contribution to the cause of Italian unification was his skill as a soldier.' Discuss this statement. (20)
NEAB

6   (a) What geographical changes took place in Germany as a result of the Vienna Settlement? (4)

   (b) Explain the reasons for the establishment of the German Confederation. (5)

   (c) To what extent was Prussia the principal beneficiary of these geographical and political changes? (7)

   (d) Did the Vienna Settlement lay the foundations for German unity? Explain your reasons fully. (9)
WJEC

7   How far would you agree that Bismarck reacted to events rather than having a long-term plan for the unification of Germany? (25)
NICCEA

8   Compare the means by which Bismarck and Cavour dealt with Austria in the unification of Germany and Italy respectively. (25)
Cambridge

Key developments

1814	Louis XVIII (Bourbon) King. Charter issued
1815	Return and defeat of Napoleon I
1824	Accession of Charles X
1830	Ordinances of St Cloud. Revolution. Abdication of Charles X. Election of Louis Philippe as King
1834	Rising in Paris, Lyons
1848	Revolution. Abdication of Louis Philippe. Second Republic proclaimed. Louis Napoleon elected President
1851	Coup d'état of Louis Napoleon
1852	Napoleon III proclaimed Emperor
1860	Introduction of liberal measures
1870	Plebiscite victory of Napoleon III. Defeat at Sedan. Revolution in Paris. Proclamation of Republic

The restored Bourbons

Louis XVIII, a Bourbon, became king in 1814, pursuing moderate policies. The **ultras**, or extreme monarchists, provoked the 'White Terror', taking revenge on revolutionaries and supporters of Napoleon. Their leader was the Comte D'Artois, the king's brother, who succeeded him as Charles X. The **Bonapartists** were inspired by Napoleon I and the **'Napoleonic Legend'**. **Republicans** defended the changes after the Revolution. After 1820, increasing ill-health, minor risings in France and the ultras pushed Louis XVIII into more extreme policies. The Comte d'Artois was able to exercise more influence.

Charles X became king in 1824 and was crowned at Reims in the traditional form. He recognised the authority of the Catholic Church, restoring the pre-revolutionary link between monarchy and Church. Emigrés (aristocratic exiles from the Revolution) were encouraged to return to France. He appointed as chief minister **Polignac**, an extreme ultra and former émigré. Charles dissolved the Chamber and, using emergency powers, issued the reactionary **Ordinances of St Cloud**. Riots in Paris developed into revolution and, when soldiers failed to restore order, Charles X **abdicated** (1830).

The 'liberal monarchy' of Louis Philippe

Why Louis Philippe?
Louis Philippe was a member of the **Orleans** branch of the royal family and had shown some sympathy to the French Revolution. A man of modest personal tastes, he seemed a middle-class citizen rather than aristocratic. The **'Citizen King'** seemed the best compromise candidate in 1830. He was an **elected** king, an important difference, and his title, 'King of the French, by the Grace of God and the will of the nation', emphasised his dependence on the agreement of the French people.

The Orleanist monarchy
Republicans, Bonapartists and **legitimists** (supporters of the Bourbons) created instability while government ministries were short-lived. Although Louis Philippe had accepted a limited monarchy he was determined to use his power to the full. His advisers and ministers, such as **Guizot**, were anti-liberal and the regime became marked by corruption and inefficiency.

The economy became more prosperous but few benefited and the government was unwilling to interfere with free trade by introducing legislation which would have protected the working classes. Guizot's response to popular dissatisfaction was 'Enrich yourselves'. When the condition of the economy worsened in the late 1840s, the government's unpopularity increased. **Socialists**, such as Blanc and Blanqui, spread their ideas of social reform, political idealism and the right to work.

Louis Napoleon, nephew of Napoleon I, was the champion of the Bonapartists and led two unsuccessful risings against Louis Philippe. The 'Napoleonic Legend' was becoming stronger and the government's efforts to defuse the situation by returning the ashes of Napoleon I for a ceremonial burial in Paris backfired by increasing Bonapartist enthusiasm.

In his foreign policy, Louis Philippe seemed more anxious to win the goodwill of other European countries, for example Britain, than to promote the interests of France. These policies increased his problems and by 1848 Louis Philippe found himself isolated in Europe and discredited in France.

In 1848, there were popular demonstrations against Louis Philippe and a move to extend the franchise caused opposition. Public meetings were banned as were protest **'banquets'** which spread anti-government propaganda. Violence spread from Paris to all parts of France. **Louis Philippe abdicated** in the face of overwhelming opposition.

The Second Republic

Louis Napoleon represented liberty to the republicans, order to monarchists, reform to socialists and sound religion to the Church. He won an overwhelming victory in the election for President of the Republic. France was still disturbed by violent protests. To restore order, censorship was restored and the franchise was limited. The constitution limited the President to one four-year term of office but Louis Napoleon campaigned for a change, allowing him to stand again. In a coup d'état (1851) he declared himself President for a further term of 10 years. He then abolished the Republic and declared himself **Emperor, Napoleon III** (1852).

The Second Empire

Napoleon III

Napoleon III was a man of many contradictions. He was authoritarian but also anxious to gain popular support. He suppressed democracy in France but supported liberal movements elsewhere in Europe. He saw himself as a man of destiny but his ideas were muddled. He tried to restore France as a great international power but succeeded only in alienating every other European country until he was completely isolated in 1870.

Napoleon III's policies

Napoleon III controlled ministers and dictated policy, but his dictatorship was not violent nor unduly repressive. Plebiscites were used to win popular support. His reign coincided with a period of prosperity. Public works helped to create full employment; interest rates remained low; and railways and heavy industry grew rapidly. Banks were founded.

After 1860 Napoleon III allowed more debate in parliament. Censorship was relaxed and public meetings were allowed. However, historians debate whether this **'Liberal Empire'** was a genuine move to a more consultative style of government or an attempt to forestall opposition. In 1870, a plebiscite confirmed Napoleon III's popularity.

Why did Napoleon III fall?

Napoleon III's failure was rooted in foreign policy. The **Crimean War**, with the peace conference at Paris (1856), was his only success abroad. In **Italy** he supported Cavour. France gained Nice and Savoy but his change of mind after the battle of Solferino offended French liberals, who supported Italian nationalism. In **Mexico** (1861), Napoleon III's scheme to create a French empire failed, making him unpopular at home and abroad.

When **Prussia** was preparing to go to war with **Austria** (1865–6), Napoleon III was misled by Bismarck into believing that France would acquire territory. The emperor assumed that he could benefit from a long war but, after Prussia's swift victory, he gained nothing. Napoleon III was outmanoeuvred again by Bismarck in the events leading to the **Franco-Prussian War** (1870). Bismarck made it appear that France was making unreasonable demands. The emperor gave in to the demands of French public opinion and declared war. The battle of **Sedan** resulted in the **abdication of Napoleon III**, the end of the Second Empire and the establishment of the Third Republic.

1 Who, in the period 1815–1870, was the most successful ruler of France? Justify your view by reference to all of the rulers of France in this period. (25)

AEB

2 'Domestically a success but internationally a failure.' To what extent would you accept this verdict on the French Second Empire? (25)

NICCEA

3 Explain the overthrow of the Bourbon monarchy in France in 1830. (25)

WJEC

4 (a) Write a sentence giving ONE way in which Charles X changed France after becoming King. (2)

(b) Write a sentence to explain the meaning of the term 'ultra'. (2)

(c) Write one or two sentences to explain why there was a revolution in France in July 1830. (3)

(d) Write one or two sentences to explain why Louis Philippe was asked to become King in 1830. (3)

(e) Write a paragraph to explain why Louis Philippe was known as the 'King of the French'. (5)

ULEAC

5 'A showman dictator.' How accurate is this view of Napoleon III? (25)

Oxford

6 Why did the France of Napoleon III become isolated in Europe by 1870? (25)

Cambridge

10 *Causes of the First World War, 1871–1914*

Key developments

1871	Franco-German Treaty at Frankfurt. France ceded Alsace-Lorraine; reparations to Germany
1879	Dual Alliance: Austria-Hungary and Germany
1882	Triple Alliance: Austria-Hungary, Germany and Italy
1891	Dual Alliance: France and Russia
1904	Anglo-French Entente
1905	Moroccan Crisis
1907	Triple Entente: Britain, France and Russia
1911	Agadir Crisis
1912–13	Balkan Wars
1914	*June:* assassination of Archduke Franz Ferdinand and wife at Sarajevo
	July: German 'blank cheque' to Austria-Hungary. Austro-Hungarian ultimatum to Serbia. Russian mobilisation. Germany declared war on Russia, France
	August: Germany invaded Belgium. Schlieffen Plan. Austria-Hungary declared war on Russia. Britain declared war on Germany, Austria-Hungary
	October/November: Austria-Hungary and Germany joined by Turkey, Bulgaria

Europe in 1870

The 1870s were a crucial decade. France continued to seek revenge for its defeat by Prussia (1870) while Bismarck relied on France not being able to gain powerful allies and on Germany not alienating other nations. The League of the Three Emperors (**Dreikaiserbund**, 1873), a loose understanding between Austria-Hungary, Germany and Russia, reassured Germany but isolated France. It appeared as if Bismarck had succeeded in dealing with France but his success was short-lived.

The **Eastern Question** continued to trouble Europe. The **Congress of Berlin** (1878) was Bismarck's attempt to solve the problem. In the short term, the major powers were satisfied with the outcome of the Congress but the agreement was illusory. The Balkans issue continued to divide Austria-Hungary and Russia, and also involved other countries.

The making of alliances

Bismarck's system of checks and balances had begun to unravel by the time of his fall (1890) and did not survive under William II. The **Dual Alliance** (1879) between Austria-Hungary and Germany became the **Triple Alliance** (1882) when Italy joined. The Reinsurance Treaty with Russia was not renewed and the Dreikaiserbund was effectively dead.

France now had a potential ally in Russia. Their **Dual Alliance** (1891) was an important change in the balance of power. The next development was an agreement between Britain and France although the **'Entente Cordiale'** (1904) was not a formal alliance and was often less than cordial. The **Anglo-Russian Entente** (1907) was followed by the **Triple Entente** (1907) of Britain, France and Russia.

International rivalries

William II was ambitious to be recognised as a major international figure and he wanted Germany to become a world rather than a European power. Vanity, inconsistency and lack of judgement made him unpredictable. There is evidence that his ministers and military advisers, including Chancellor von Bulow, Holstein and von Schlieffen, were able to take advantage of his ambitions to persuade him into actions that threatened peace.

The **Navy Laws** (1898 and 1900) signalled Germany's determination to rival Britain. In turn, Britain was determined to preserve its supremacy at sea and the outcome was a naval arms race. Continental powers enlarged their armies. More modern weapons were introduced and aggressive military strategies were planned.

William II's telegram to Kruger, President of the Transvaal, congratulating him on the defeat of the Jameson Raid (1896) was seen by Britain as interference in its imperial interests. The proposal to build a 'Berlin-Baghdad railway' was interpreted by Russia as German support for the Ottoman empire and by Britain as threatening the stability of the Middle East. The visit of the Kaiser to **Tangier** (1905) and the despatch of the gunboat to **Agadir** (1911) signalled a German challenge to British and French interests in North Africa. The outcome was a diplomatic defeat for Germany and personal humiliation for William II. He strengthened rather than weakened the Anglo-French entente and increased their suspicion of Germany.

Crises in the Balkans

The fragile peace in the Balkans ended at the beginning of the twentieth century. Germany's intention to play a role became a new complicating factor. Austria-Hungary had controlled Bosnia since 1878 but now wished to annex it in an attempt to stamp out dissent within its own borders and to prevent the enlargement of Serbia and the Ottoman empire (1908). Russia's position as the protector of the Slavs was threatened while Germany saw the opportunity to display its power in backing Austria-Hungary although it had no direct interests in the Balkans.

The immediate outcome favoured Austria-Hungary and Germany, which had recovered some of the prestige lost in North Africa, but the long-term effect was to damage the chances of peace. William II and his ministers believed that because Russia had withdrawn, France had been unwilling to risk war and Britain had stood aloof, they would do so again.

Two **Balkan Wars** (1912–13) broke out and showed that Serbia could make common cause with other small countries, such as Bulgaria and Romania. A wider conflict was avoided only when the members of the rival alliance stepped back from the brink.

The 1914 Crisis

In June 1914 the Archduke **Franz Ferdinand**, heir to the Austro-Hungarian empire, and his wife were assassinated by a Bosnian Serb in **Sarajevo**, capital of Bosnia. The Austro-Hungarian government blamed Serbia and it is very likely that senior figures in Serbia were aware of the plot. An ultimatum was issued which would virtually have ended Serbian independence and it is probable that the ultimatum was intended to be rejected in order to give Austria-Hungary a justification for war.

Serbia, encouraged by Russia, was willing to be conciliatory and Britain attempted to mediate. However, Austria-Hungary's determination to crush Serbia was stiffened when it received a 'blank cheque' of support for its actions from Germany. Historians debate whether Germany intended a general war at this time and it is likely that it envisaged a localised conflict between Austria-Hungary and Serbia, as a decisive end to a long-running regional dispute.

Austria-Hungary declared war on **Serbia**. **Germany** declared war on **Russia**, then on **France**. Its military strategy was based on the Schlieffen Plan which involved an attack on France through Belgium. German leaders believed that Britain would not go to war merely because of a promise made in 1839 to protect Belgian neutrality. Historians debate whether British ministers made clear to Germany how they would react, but **Britain** decided to meet its obligations to **Belgium**. Within six weeks of Sarajevo, every major European power was at war.

In 1918 it seemed clear that Germany had caused the war. This certainty was later moderated when historians suggested more complex interpretations. While not exonerating Germany, they pointed out other factors, such as the rival alliances and the armaments race, as causes of the war.

In the 1960s **Fischer**, a German historian, claimed that Germany's 'Grasp for World Power' was primarily responsible and saw a continuity between German policy before 1914 with Hitler's policies in the 1930s. This began a lively debate about German war guilt, some supporting Fischer and others criticising his view for being too simplistic.

If you need to revise this subject more thoroughly, see the relevant topic in the *Letts A-level European History Study Guide*.

1 'Those seeking to discover the men responsible for starting the First World War need look no further than Berlin.' Would you accept this judgement? (25)

NICCEA

2 Was the system of alliances and ententes mainly responsible for the outbreak of war in 1914? Explain your answer fully. (25)

WJEC

3 To what extent was German foreign policy between 1895 and 1914 'dangerously aggressive'? (25)

Oxford

4 In what ways did events in (a) Morocco and (b) the Balkans in 1912–14 play a part in the outbreak of war? (15)

ULEAC

5 Why did instability in the Balkans lead to the outbreak of a general European war in 1914? (25)

AEB

6 Why did diplomacy not resolve the European crisis of 1914? (25)

Cambridge

Key developments

1905	Revolution in St Petersburg
1906	Russian constitution. First Duma. Stolypin Prime Minister
1914	Outbreak of First World War
1917	February Revolution. Provisional government. Kerensky Prime Minister
	October Revolution. Bolshevik government. Lenin's leadership
1921	New Economic Policy
1922	Stalin Secretary-General
1924	Death of Lenin
1925	Stalin's policy of 'Socialism in One Country'. Fall of Trotsky
1928	First Five-Year Plan
1933	Second Five-Year Plan
1935	Purges. Treason trials
1938	Third Five-Year Plan
1941	Attack on USSR by Germany

Tsarist Russia

The 1905 Revolution
Nicholas II believed in absolute monarchy and saw political concessions as weakness. Defeat in a war with Japan (1904–5) unleashed popular discontent with the government. However, the army remained loyal to the tsar and suppressed the risings, centred on **St Petersburg** and **Moscow**.

Russia to 1914
The tsar was persuaded to concede a limited measure of reform. The franchise was extended although only to a minority of the working classes. A constitution was issued which established a **Duma**, or parliament. Unlike the First and Second Dumas (1905 and 1907), which were dissolved by the tsar, the Third Duma (1907–12) introduced some reforms. **Stolypin** (Prime Minister, 1906–11) introduced some economic changes but his murder in 1911 was followed by a return to reactionary policies.

The effects of the First World War
The inefficiency of the Russian army had disastrous results, leading to heavy defeats. In 1915 Nicholas II took personal control but only to demonstrate his military incompetence. The news of casualties and defeat, often relayed by deserting soldiers, had profound effects on the civilian population. Strikes paralysed Russia. Disillusion led to resentment against the tsar, who was seen as the primary cause of Russia's troubles. Faced with widespread disorder, **Nicholas II abdicated** (1917).

The 1917 Revolutions

The revolution in **February 1917** took Lenin and the Bolsheviks by surprise. Liberals took the initiative with Prince Lvov at the head of a Provisional government. **Kerensky**, a democratic socialist revolutionary, later became Prime Minister of a moderate government. Lenin promised **'Peace, Land and Bread'** and his supporters organised workers' 'soviets' in factories and in the army. The pressures were irresistible and the Bolsheviks seized power in **October 1917**. They did not exercise full control until the end of the civil war against the Whites (1920).

The communists in power

Lenin
Lenin's unwillingness to compromise with other communists kept the Bolsheviks as a minority group. His rapid organisation and his determination were largely instrumental in bringing the Bolsheviks to power in October 1917.

The Red Guard, a militia, and the Cheka, a political police force, suppressed any opposition, real or suspected. Other political parties were banned. The workers' soviets were controlled by the **Supreme Congress of Soviets**, dominated by the Bolsheviks.

War Communism was introduced in which agricultural produce was confiscated. Peasants killed their animals rather than have them seized and they did not plant crops from which they would gain nothing. Lenin then initiated the **New Economic Policy (NEP)** which modified the communist insistence on state control. Peasants and larger landowners were allowed to keep some of their produce for private sales while small industrialists and traders were tolerated.

In 1922 the creation of the Union of Soviet Socialist Republics (USSR) was announced, formalising the link between Russia and the other republics which it controlled. Russia remained the most important state but from this date it is more correct to talk about the USSR, the Soviet economy, the Soviet government, etc.

Stalin

Stalin became **Secretary of the Communist Party** (1922). After the death of Lenin (1924) his main rival was Trotsky. Trotsky's belief in spreading communism outside the USSR (**'permanent revolution'**) distinguished him from Stalin whose priority was consolidating communism in the USSR (**'socialism in one country'**). Stalin won the struggle for power. Trotsky was driven into exile and later assassinated (1940).

Stalin and the economy. Stalin imposed the policy of **collectivisation** which created large state-controlled farms. Many kulaks were killed, others were deported to distant regions to be enslaved in labour camps or forced to work in state factories.

Stalin cancelled Lenin's NEP in the first **Five-Year Plan** (1928), concentrating on heavy industry. Workers were forced to achieve continually higher targets by a mixture of rewards and punishment. The second Five-Year Plan (1933) allowed for some limited production of consumer goods but the third Five-Year Plan (1938) returned to the emphasis on heavy industry.

Terror. Stalin used terror against anyone who was a critic or a suspected critic from every section of society. From 1935 there were trials in Moscow in which eminent members of the party, including close associates of Lenin and leaders of the 1917 Revolution, were prosecuted. Army generals and other officers were executed, virtually destroying the officer corps.

Propaganda portrayed Stalin as the great leader who was concerned for his people and on whom everything depended, and there is little doubt that he enjoyed the overwhelming support of the people in spite of his brutal methods.

By 1939, Stalin had brought about changes far more wide-ranging than had Lenin but historians debate how far he had positive achievements. The **'destalinisation'** which followed Stalin's death (1953) and the more recent disintegration of the USSR have led both Soviet and western historians to be more critical of the effects of his policies.

Stalin and Hitler. For much of the inter-war period, the USSR was isolated from international diplomacy. In the mid-1930s, Stalin began to take more interest in European affairs, joining the League of Nations (1934) and sending forces to fight in the Spanish Civil War.

Hitler's ambitions persuaded Stalin that he should seek an agreement with Germany. The **German-Soviet Pact** (1939) bought time for Stalin, but Hitler then launched **Operation Barbarossa** against the USSR (1941). It was to be a war which was to test Stalin's powers of leadership and drain the human and economic resources of his people before victory was achieved.

1 'Terminally ill in 1914' or 'Killed in action in the First World War'. Which seems to you the more appropriate diagnosis of the fate of Tsarism? (25)
NICCEA

2 Is 'terror' a sufficient explanation of Stalin's pre-eminence in the USSR in the years to 1941? (25)
Cambridge

3 Why did the Tsarist regime survive in Russia in 1905, but not in 1917? (25)
Oxford

4 Assess (a) the similarities and (b) the differences between Tsarist and Bolshevik rule in Russia in the period c.1900–1929. (25)
AEB

5 (a) Identify the main political parties in 1917. (4)

(b) Explain the policies of the Bolsheviks on war and land reform. (5)

(c) To what extent were Bolshevik policies attractive to the Russian people in 1917? (7)

(d) Was the weakness of the Whites the main cause of the Bolshevik victory in the Russian Civil War? Explain your answer fully. (9)
WJEC

6 Why did Stalin end Lenin's New Economic Policy? How successful were Stalin's own economic policies in the years 1928–41? (15)
ULEAC

12 Nazism in Germany, 1919–39

Key developments

1918	Defeat in First World War
1919	Weimar constitution. Treaty of Versailles
1923	Stresemann Chancellor; then Foreign Minister. Nazi putsch at Munich. Hitler imprisoned
1929	Death of Stresemann. Wall Street Crash
1930	Nazis second largest party in Reichstag
1933	Hitler appointed Chancellor. Enabling Act
1934	'Night of the Long Knives', purge of SA
1935	Nuremberg Laws; anti-Jewish legislation
1936	German army entered demilitarised Rhineland
1938	Munich agreement. 'Kristallnacht'
1939	Occupation of all Czechoslovakia. Nazi-Soviet Pact. Invasion of Poland. Outbreak of Second World War

The Weimar Republic

The Weimar **constitution** was very democratic. The President was directly elected and normally exercised limited powers. There was universal franchise for men and women for the Reichstag (parliament), with secret ballot and proportional representation. However, there were many small parties, some of them anti-democratic, and a succession of unstable coalitions.

The Weimar Republic had to accept a dictated peace in the **Treaty of Versailles** (1919). Germany lost territories in Europe and overseas and its armed forces were severely limited. The **War Guilt Clause** affirmed 'the aggression of Germany and her allies'. A few years after Versailles, a commission decided that Germany should pay reparations of more than £6 billion.

Instability and crisis
Military defeat and Versailles were regarded as a **'stab in the back'** by the Germans who sought scapegoats for their troubles. The Germans suffered from **extreme inflation**. Violent strikes threatened disorder while extreme political groups struggled for power.

The Weimar Republic survived these dangers and the 1920s were a period of recovery. Led by **Stresemann**, (Chancellor, then Foreign Secretary) Germany's economy began to recover. The Dawes Plan and the Young Plan revised the reparations. The Locarno Treaty (1925) saw a relaxation of relations with France. Germany entered the League of Nations with a permanent seat on the Council which reflected its acceptance as a major European power.

However, after **Stresemann's death** and the **Wall Street Crash** (1929) Germany returned to the political instability and the economic problems of the early post-war period.

Germany as a Nazi state

Hitler
Born in Austria, Hitler fought in the German army in the First World War. Like many other ex-soldiers, he was attracted to extreme political groups after the war. His oratory and racist views made him the leader of the Nazi Party.

Hitler advocated the need for a strong leader (**Führer**) and gained support by expressing in extreme but simple terms the anger and frustration of Germans against those whom they blamed for their problems, especially the Jews.

He adapted his methods after the Munich putsch (1923). Although his supporters, led by the SA, used violence against opponents, he made the Nazi Party into a mass movement which would gain power through the electoral system. The vote for the Nazi Party grew rapidly from 3 per cent (1928) to 37 per cent (1932) and 44 per cent in 1933.

The Nazis gain power

President Hindenburg supported right-wing groups and he allowed successive chancellors to govern by emergency decree. None of the other politicians could form a stable government but Hitler refused to join any coalition which the Nazis did not control. Ultimately senior politicians, generals and industrialists were convinced that Hitler could be controlled and he became **Chancellor** (1933).

One month after he became Chancellor, the Reichstag building was destroyed by a fire which was blamed by the Nazis on the communists and Hitler used it to justify his seizure of complete power. The Enabling Act suspended the constitution. Other political parties were banned; freedom of the press and of public assembly was limited. When Hindenburg died (1934), Hitler combined the offices of **President and Chancellor**.

The Nazis in power

Every section of society came under the control of the Nazi Party. The Labour Front replaced trade unions. Schools emphasised Nazi theories and a racist form of German history. The Hitler Youth and the League of German Maidens indoctrinated young people. Publications were heavily censored. The SS controlled the police while judges were expected to support the party. Hitler crushed any rival groups within the Nazi Party. To persuade Germans that the Nazis were respectable, he destroyed the SA, and their leaders were killed in **'The Night of the Long Knives'**.

The **Four-Year Plan** (1936) used state planning to prepare for war. 'Autarky' promoted self-sufficiency. However, the Nazi control of the economy was never as complete as that of the communists in the USSR.

Concentration camps were set up for 'anti-social' people who included homosexuals, freemasons, members of small religious groups, communists and, most numerously, Jews. **Anti-semitism** was a major force in Nazism. Anti-Jewish measures increased with the **Nuremberg Laws** (1935) stripping the Jews of their civil rights. 'Kristallnacht' (Night of Broken Glass, 1938) saw widespread violence against Jewish shops and synagogues. In the **'Final Solution'**, millions of Jews from Germany, and then from most of the countries which Germany conquered, were killed in concentration camps in an attempt at total extermination.

Hitler's war

Hitler was determined to retrieve the losses of Versailles. Not only was this supported enthusiastically by Germans, but by 1933 there was a growing feeling in the rest of western Europe that Versailles had been unfair, forcing Germany to concede too much. The armed forces were increased; Germany withdrew from the League of Nations but secured its agreement to the recovery of the Saar.

When the **Rhineland** was reoccupied (1936), the unwillingness of Britain and France to force Germany's withdrawal encouraged Hitler to go further. The **'Anschluss'** united Austria and Germany. Hitler then used the grievances of the German-speaking inhabitants of the Sudetenland as an excuse to press for the partition of **Czechoslovakia**. Britain, supported by France agreed at **Munich** (1938), but Hitler then increased his demands to include the incorporation of all Czechoslovakia. Britain and France again agreed.

Germany's non-aggression pact with the USSR preceded the attack on **Poland** in 1939. Britain and France would not concede again to Hitler. War broke out immediately and ended in 1945 with the complete defeat of Nazi Germany and the suicide of Hitler.

If you need to revise this subject more thoroughly, see the relevant topic in the *Letts* A-level *European History Study Guide*.

1   How far was Hitler's accession to office in 1933 the result of the weakness of the Weimar Republic rather than the strength of the Nazi movement?   (25)
Oxford

2   Read the following extract from *Hitler and Stalin: Parallel Lives* by A. Bullock and then answer the questions which follow.

'Looking at the broader spectrum of popular opinion … most observers agreed that during the 1930s there were certain features of the regime [in Germany] which were viewed positively.'

(a)   Why, by the mid-1930s, was Hitler's regime viewed 'positively'?   (8)

(b)   How effectively did the regime maintain its control over Germany to 1939?   (12)
NEAB

3   (a)   Identify the anti-German elements of the Versailles Treaty.   (4)

(b)   Explain how these elements would antagonise the Germans.   (5)

(c)   To what extent did Hitler rely on German dislike of the Treaty to achieve power?   (7)

(d)   Was this dislike the main basis of support for the Nazis between 1933 and 1939? Explain your answer fully.   (9)
WJEC

4   'A noble experiment with positive achievements.' 'Hated by every powerful group in Germany.' Consider these judgements on the Weimar Republic.   (25)
Cambridge

5   To what extent, by 1938, had the domestic policies of the Nazi regime solved the internal problems which it had inherited from the Weimar Republic?   (25)
AEB

6   Would you agree with the view that Hitler's conduct of foreign policy was purely 'opportunist'? Explain your answer fully.   (25)
WJEC

Social and economic ideas of the Chartists

1   Study Documents I, II and III below and then answer questions (a) to (e) which follow.

Document I

It seems to me that a *Parliament* resolved on consulting the interests of the many and not of the few, might, in an infinite variety of ways, *increase the comfort* and exalt the character of the human race.

5   Repeal of … *taxes upon articles of consumption* would … [make] … necessaries and comforts … more abundant and … within the reach of all classes …

Employment might be made abundant … There cannot be good wages when the *supply of labour* greatly exceeds the demand. How to prevent the latter evil is the principal matter … for consideration. In the first place the labour market may be relieved … from women and children, for if the earnings of the head of a family be not sufficient … let assistance be

10   given by the public, in order that children … may be sent to school, and the wife be kept at home to attend to domestic affairs.

Secondly … the cheapening of … necessaries will leave more money to be expended on manufactured goods …

Thirdly, each trade and employment can be relieved … of its superfluous hands by a

15   careful and judicious encouragement of emigration …

No expense should be spared on the part of the government to establish colonies in a proper manner … New sources of commerce and trade might be thrown open for us, and thus a double benefit be obtained …

Fourthly, great *public works* could be set on foot by the encouragement of the

20   government … This would create permanent employment.

An extract from the newspaper *The Charter*, 25 August 1839

Document II

Your *petitioners* would direct the attention of your honourable House to the great disparity existing between the wages of the producing millions, and the salaries of those whose comparative usefulness ought to be questioned …

Notwithstanding the wretched and unparalleled condition of the people, your Honourable

5   House has manifested no disposition to curtail the expenses of the State, to diminish taxation or promote general prosperity …

The hours of labour, particularly of the factory workers, are protected beyond the limits of endurance, and the wages earned … are inadequate.

Thomas Duncombe, presenting the second Chartist petition in the House of Commons, 2 May 1842

Document III

There has been a constant and systematic attempt … to represent the Government as being able to do, and as bound to attempt, that which no government ever attempted; and instead of the Government being represented, as is the truth, as being supported by the people, it has been treated as if the government supported the people … as if the Government

5   possessed some mine of wealth – some extraordinary means of satisfying the wants of the people.

T B Macaulay, in the House of Commons, 5 May 1842

41

(a) In the context of the Documents, explain what was meant by:

    (i) 'taxes upon articles of consumption' (line 4);

    (ii) 'supply of labour' (lines 6–7); and

    (iii) 'public works' (line 19).   (3)

(b) What strategies, according to Document I, should be followed by 'Parliament' (line 1) to 'increase the comfort' (line 2) of the British population?   (4)

(c) Noting the language, tone and content of Document II, comment on the manner in which the 'petitioners' (line 1) presented their case to Parliament.   (4)

(d) Explain the line of argument advanced by Macaulay (Document III) in response to the proposals made in Document I and to the arguments advanced in Document II.   (6)

(e) Using these Documents, and your own knowledge, explain why Chartism attracted so much support in the years 1839–42.   (8)

ULEAC

Lloyd George and social reforms, 1908–12

2   Read the extracts below, and then answer the questions which follow.

Extract A: From the *Old Age Pensions Act*, 1908, promoted through Parliament by David Lloyd George, Chancellor of the Exchequer in the Liberal Government.

The statutory conditions for the receipt of an old age pension by any person are:

(1) the person must have attained the age of seventy.

(2) The person must satisfy the pension authorities that for at least twenty years up to the date of the receipt of any sum on account of a pension he has been a British subject, and has had his residence … in the United Kingdom.

(3) The person must satisfy the pension authorities that his yearly means as calculated under this Act do not exceed thirty-one pounds ten shillings.

Extract B: From *Edwardian England*, by Donald Read, 1972.

'God bless that Lord George' was the cry at … post offices when the first pensions were paid at the start of 1909. Old-age pensions were one social reform generally and immediately popular among the Edwardian working class. Over 400,000 pensions were soon being distributed in England and Wales to nearly 45 per cent of the population aged over 70. Outdoor poor relief for this age group became almost unnecessary, a sign that the new payments were successfully serving a major social need.

Extract C: From the *National Insurance Act*, 1911, promoted through Parliament by Lloyd George.

Every workman who, having been employed in a trade, is unemployed … shall be entitled … to receive payments (in this Act referred to as 'unemployment benefit') at weekly or other prescribed intervals at such rates and for such periods as are authorised … The sums required for the payment of unemployment benefit under this Act shall be derived partly from contributions by workmen in the insured trades and partly from contributions from employers of such workmen and partly from moneys provided by Parliament … A contribution shall be made in each year out of moneys provided by Parliament equal to one-third of the total contributions received from employers and workmen during that year.

Extract D: From a speech by Lloyd George, made in Kennington, London on 13 July 1912.

Here is this great <u>National Insurance scheme</u> which touches every household, every industry, every trade, and all our interests. If there are slips and little stumblings, remember it is the first time that the nation has been mobilised. What for? Not to wage war upon their fellow-men, not to march into the territories of people who are flesh of our flesh and blood of our blood, to ravage and destroy, but for the purpose of securing health, for securing plenty, and for driving away the privation and hunger that have invaded millions of homes …

They [the Act's opponents] have assailed it bitterly with misrepresentation, with falsehoods, direct, unqualified, which they have refused to withdraw when their attention has been called to it … when insults hurtle through the air, I can always see a vision on the horizon that sustains me … I can see the Old Age Pension Act, the National Insurance Act, and many another Act in their trail descending, like breezes from the hills of my native land, and sweeping into the mist-laden valleys, and clearing the gloom away until the rays of God's sun have pierced the narrowest window.

(a) Consult Extracts B and D.

With reference to these extracts, and to your own knowledge, explain what was meant at the time by the following phrases, which are underlined in the extracts.

(i) 'Outdoor poor relief' (Extract B)

(ii) 'National Insurance scheme' (Extract D) (6)

(b) Consult Extracts B and D.

How might the determination of Lloyd George to reduce poverty in Britain be inferred from these extracts? (4)

(c) Consult all four extracts and use your own knowledge.

How extensively in the period 1906–1914 did the Liberal governments increase state responsibility for the welfare of British citizens? (10)

NEAB

Hitler and Germany, 1933–45: Führer power

3

Document A

I had a long talk with State secretary Lammers about Schacht. He said the Führer found it so difficult to make decisions about personnel. He always hoped that things would sort themselves out on their own. A decision had not yet been made because the Führer was not satisfied with the nomination of only one state secretary and would prefer to appoint a
5 minister. He kept hoping that the question of personnel would solve itself.

Diary entry of the Lord Mayor of Hamburg, autumn 1937

Document B

The office of Führer has developed out of the National Socialist movement. In its origins it is not a state office. The office of Führer has grown out of the movement into the Reich. The position of Führer combines in itself all sovereign power of the Reich: all public power in the state, as in the movement, is derived from the Führer's power. If we wish to define
5 political power in the völkisch Reich correctly, we must not speak of 'state power' but of 'Führer power'. For it is not the state as an impersonal entity which is the source of political

power, but rather political power is given to the Führer as the executor of the nation's common will. 'Führer power' is comprehensive and total; it unites within itself all means of creative political activity; it embraces all spheres of national life; it includes all national
10 comrades who are bound to the Führer in loyalty and obedience. 'Führer power' is not restricted by safeguards and controls, and by vested individual rights, but rather it is free and independent, exclusive and unlimited.

> Ernst Rudolf Huber, leading constitutional theorist of the Third Reich,
> *The Constitutional Law of the German Reich*, 1939

Document C
In the twelve years of his rule in Germany Hitler produced the biggest confusion in government that has ever existed in a civilised state. During his period of government, he removed from the organisation of the state all clarity of leadership. It was not all laziness or an excessive degree of tolerance which led the otherwise so energetic and forceful Hitler to
5 tolerate this real witch's cauldron of struggles for position and conflicts over competence. It was intentional. With this technique he systematically disorganised the upper echelons of the Reich leadership in order to develop and further the authority of his own will until it became a despotic tyranny.

> Otto Dietrich, *Twelve Years with Hitler*, 1955

Document D
In 1935 Hitler kept to a reasonably ordered daily routine. Gradually this broke down. He disliked the study of documents. I sometimes secured decisions from him, even ones about important matters, without his ever asking to see the relevant files. He took the view that many things sorted themselves out on their own if one did not interfere. But the question
5 was how did they sort themselves out? The Party leaders found it easiest to get something out of him. If they belonged to the top ranks they could always come to lunch. It is not surprising that the State offices were outmanoeuvred. He let people tell him the things he wanted to hear, everything else he rejected. One still sometimes hears the view that Hitler would have done the right thing if people surrounding him had not kept him wrongly
10 informed. Hitler refused to let himself be informed.

> The memoirs of Fritz Wiedemann, one of Hitler's adjutants, 1965

Document E
In the eyes of the people Hitler was the Leader who watched over the nation day and night. This was hardly so. But Hitler's lax scheduling could be regarded as a lifestyle characteristic of the artistic temperament. He often allowed a problem to mature during the weeks when he seemed entirely taken up with trivial matters. Then, after the 'sudden
5 insight' came, he would spend a few days of intensive work giving final shape to his solution. Once he had come to a decision, he relapsed again into his idleness.

After 1933 there quickly formed various factions that held divergent views, spied on each other, and held each other in contempt. A mixture of scorn and dislike became the prevailing mood within the party. Each new dignitary rapidly gathered a circle of intimates
10 around him.

As an intellectual, Goebbels looked down on the crude philistines of the leading group in Munich, who for their part made fun of the conceited academic's literary ambitions. Goering considered neither the Munich philistines nor Goebbels sufficiently aristocratic for him, and therefore, avoided all social relations with them; whereas Himmler, filled with
15 the élitist missionary zeal of the SS (which for a time expressed itself in a bias for the sons of princes and counts), felt far superior to all the others. Hitler, too, had his retinue, which

went everywhere with him. Its membership, consisting of chauffeurs, the photographer, his pilot and secretaries, remained always the same.

Albert Speer, *Inside the Third Reich*, 1970

(a) Explain briefly the following references:

    (i) 'Schacht' (Document A, line 1);   (1)

    (ii) 'Goebbels looked down on the crude philistines' (Document E, line 11);   (2)

    (iii) 'the élitist missionary zeal of the SS' (Document E, line 15).   (1)

(b) What was the nature and theory of 'Führer power' as revealed in Document B?   (3)

(c) How convincing is Speer's description in Document E of the part played by 'rival factions' in the Nazi leadership?   (4)

(d) How far do Documents A, D and E challenge the view expressed in Document C about Hitler's style of leadership?   (6)

(e) Using these documents, and any other evidence known to you, examine the propaganda image of the Nazi state as a centrally directed, ruthless efficient machine.   (8)

Cambridge

German unification, c.1862–c.1871: the Hohenzollern candidature

4 Answer ALL the questions relating to the following documents.

Document A: (Charles Antony of Hohenzollern-Sigmaringen to Bismarck, 25 February 1870).

Heart and feeling tell me that acceptance of this throne would be a hazardous venture. Only a character steeled through many-sided experiences, great self-control and a thoroughly trained political understanding would be appropriate to the execution of such a task. My son has never had the opportunity to afford proof of those characteristics.

The acceptance of this crown would represent, on the one hand, an historical turning-point and show, on the other, a supreme consciousness of Prussia's political power.

In a dynasty which represents the centre of gravity of central Europe and whose Branches might blossom on the Black Sea and beyond the Pyrenees … there rests a high mission, willed by providence, and a call to be fit to govern the most heterogeneous [diverse] elements.

These fleeting observations are only brief intimations of the view I entertain, namely that no one except his Majesty, the King, can speak the deciding word …

Document B: (Bismarck to William I, King of Prussia, 9 March 1870).

I am of the opinion that it would serve Prussian and German state interests … The Spaniards would have a feeling of gratitude towards Germany, if they are rescued from the state of anarchy into which a people predominantly monarchist in sentiment threatens to sink because it lacks a king. [Marginal note by William: "This feeling, this sympathy on the part of a nation which for the last forty years has wantonly proceeded from one revolution to another, seems to me to be highly debatable."]

For Germany it is desirable to have on the one side of France a country on whose sympathies we can rely and with whose feelings France is obliged to reckon. [Marginal note by William: "How long would these sympathies last?"] … Just as in Spain scant respect for the ruling house has paralysed the forces of the nation for centuries, so with us pride in an illustrious dynasty has been a powerful moral impetus to the development of Prussia's power in Germany ... I feel a personal need to make it plain by the present humble memorandum that if the outcome is a refusal the responsibility will not lie at my door, especially if in a near or remote future historians and public opinion were to investigate into the grounds which have led to a rejection. [Marginal note by William: "... I have strong objections to the acceptance of the Spanish crown ... and would only consent if he regarded this act as a definite vocation. In these circumstances I am unable to advise the Hereditary Prince to such an act."]

Document C: (Charles Antony to his son Leopold, 5 June 1870).

This may *perhaps* be the last time you salute your native town and homeland for some while. I have neither the will nor the power to think about it.

   ... The King is in agreement with us, that is, he accommodates himself to the political constraint of Bismarck. Had we refused, we should have had to pay for it; for the question of the Spanish throne is a prime factor in Bismarck's political calculations ...

Document D: (William I in conversation with Count Waldersee, military attaché, 8 July 1870, from Waldersee's memoirs published in 1922–23).

"We suddenly find ourselves in the middle of a very serious situation ... This is Bismarck's fault. I have never directly or officially dealt with anyone about it nor have I bound myself to anything. I can refer the French Government only to the Hohenzollern Princes and shall exercise no influence over them – so, let events find us prepared!" (These words were spoken with great emphasis.)

Document E: (Extract from the diary of Baroness Spitzemberg, the wife of the Württemburg Ambassador in Berlin, 16 July 1870).

There would have been little inclination in south Germany to wage a dynastic war for the Hohenzollerns. The moderation, on the other hand, with which Prussia has acted in this question has stolen all our hearts. Her moderation was almost humiliating to her pride. One thing I hope and long for, that we Württemburgers should be true to our national duty to the last extreme and rather perish with honour than live by the grace of our hereditary enemy.

(i)   Comment on the forms of primary evidence represented in the documents.   (10)

(ii) Discuss the evidence in Document A and Document C of Charles Antony's attitude towards the Spanish candidature.   (10)

(iii) How far do Documents B, C and D throw light on the relationship between Bismarck and William I?   (15)

(iv) What evidence do the documents offer on the relationship between monarchy and nationalism in the period?   (15)

NICCEA

Answers

1 THE AGE OF REFORM

Question 1

Examiner's tip The keyword in this question is 'liberal'. The question requires you to make a judgement in relation to it and you will therefore need to have a definition in mind. You will also need to weigh the evidence on both sides of the question.

After the suicide of Castlereagh in 1822, Lord Liverpool appointed Canning as Foreign Secretary. At about the same time, Peel replaced Sidmouth as Home Secretary, Robinson became Chancellor of the Exchequer and Huskisson President of the Board of Trade. This group of new ministers came to be known as the Liberal Tories. Their liberalism was, however, to modern eyes limited.

Examiner's tip This opening sets the scene by explaining who the Liberal Tories were and outlines the basic argument for the essay. An alternative would have been to define 'liberal', but this is not essential, provided your interpretation becomes clear in the course of the essay. Whichever sort of opening you use, keep it brief!

Undoubtedly they were liberal by contrast with their immediate predecessors. The post-war Tory ministry, faced with distress and discontent, had followed a policy of repression, symbolised by Peterloo and the Six Acts. By 1822, trade was recovering and the fear of revolution was receding. It was possible for the Liberal Tories to adopt a policy of moderate reform, which is their chief claim to be called liberal.

Peel, the new Home Secretary, turned his attention to reform of the penal code and the prisons. The savage criminal code was moderated so that the death penalty was abolished for over 100 offences. This had the beneficial effect of making juries more willing to convict offenders for lesser offences. By the Gaols Act of 1823 a number of urgently needed improvements in prison conditions were introduced: for example, women officers for women prisoners, wages for jailers instead of fees, regular visits by doctors and chaplains. The reforms were, however, limited to the larger gaols; conditions in many smaller prisons remained terrible. Finally, in 1829, Peel set up the Metropolitan Police Force. This was limited to London, but its success led to the formation of similar forces throughout the country in the following 20 years. The overall effect of Peel's reforms was the establishment of a more humane and more efficient system for the administration and enforcement of the criminal law. Much of this work was based on the ideas of humanitarian reformers such as Sir Samuel Romilly and Elizabeth Fry. Peel's acceptance of their ideas may be regarded as liberal by the standards of his time.

So too may Huskisson's move towards free trade, an idea which was to become one of the hallmarks of nineteenth-century liberalism. Working with Robinson at the Exchequer, he reduced import duties (the general duty on manufactured goods was lowered from 50 per cent to 20 per cent), relaxed the Navigation Laws and secured the passing of the Reciprocity of Duties Act. He also modified the Corn Laws by the introduction of a Sliding Scale in 1828, though there was, of course, no thought of repealing them.

Three other important reforms should be mentioned as further evidence for the liberalism of the Liberal Tories. In 1824 the Combination Acts, which had made the formation of trade unions illegal since 1799, were repealed. In 1828 the Test and Corporation Acts, which prevented Nonconformists from holding public office, were repealed. And in 1829 Catholic emancipation was achieved by the Catholic Relief Act.

These three paragraphs offer a lot of relevant factual information; but equally important is the fact that the reforms listed are explicitly offered as evidence to support the label 'Liberal Tories'. However, the Examiner is still waiting for justification of the candidate's claim that their liberalism was limited.

This is an impressive catalogue of reform, particularly by contrast with the preceding decade, and it provides a strong case for regarding the Tory governments of the 1820s as liberal. This is not, however, the whole story. The repeal of the Combination Acts was followed in 1825 by an Amending Act, which effectively deprived trade unions of the power to strike. The repeal of the Test and Corporation Acts merely made permanent rights which the Nonconformists had for long been granted by annual indemnity acts. Catholic emancipation was accepted by Wellington (who was Prime Minister at the time) and Peel not as a matter of principle, but because they reluctantly came to the conclusion that civil war in Ireland was likely if they did not. Moreover, it split the Tory Party and led to the fall of the Tory government in 1830. This in turn paved the way for the one major reform which the Tories were unwilling even to contemplate: parliamentary reform.

The opposition of the Liberal Tories to parliamentary reform and, until their hand was forced, to Catholic emancipation, is proof that they were not liberals in the modern sense. On the other hand, the work of Peel and Huskisson shows a willingness to reform which distinguishes them from the ministers of 1812–22. In many ways, the modern overtones of the word 'liberal' are misleading; perhaps the alternative term, 'enlightened Tories', is a better description of them.

The last two paragraphs lift the essay to a higher grade. Most answers will set out factual material on Peel and Huskisson, but in this part of the essay the better candidate puts the case against the label 'liberal' and thus shows the critical skill needed to make a balanced judgement in the conclusion.

Question 2

The key word in the question is 'inconsistency'. You therefore need to identify the main issues over which Peel seems to have changed his mind and consider whether there is any defence for his actions, as this answer does.

In 1846 Disraeli accused Peel of betraying the party which had brought him to power: 'Let men stand by the principle by which they rise – right or wrong'. To Peel's critics, the repeal of the Corn Laws was the final act of treachery in a career in which he had already gone against Tory principles over 'cash and Catholics'. On these issues Peel appeared inconsistent. Can it be argued, however, that there was an underlying consistency in his political outlook?

The first issue over which he offended many Tories was the resumption of cash payments, which he, as chairman of the Bullion Committee, recommended in 1819. This led to a fall in agricultural prices, to the disadvantage of Tory landowners with high mortgages, while benefiting London financial interests and exporters. This is not really an example of inconsistency on Peel's part, but it did sow the seeds of suspicion of this son of a middle-class industrialist among the aristocratic landowners who dominated the Tory Party.

There is, however, a strong case for accusing Peel of inconsistency over Catholic emancipation in 1829. The Tory Party had always been strongly anti-Catholic and Peel had made great play of his staunch Protestantism in his early years as an MP. Indeed, it was a major reason for his rise within the party. His acceptance of Catholic emancipation therefore came as a shock to many Tories and contributed greatly to the break-up of the party in 1829–30. Yet his behaviour can be defended: he did not support Catholic emancipation as such but came to the conclusion after the County Clare election that the threat of civil war in Ireland made it necessary. The maintenance of law and order was as much a Tory principle as support for the Protestant establishment. On this matter Peel put the national interest above his own views, though Wellington had to persuade him not to resign on the issue.

His third great betrayal (in Tory eyes) was the repeal of the Corn Laws in 1846. Here too there seems to be a good case for charging him with inconsistency. The Corn Laws were a Tory measure, introduced by them in 1815 and regarded by the landowning class as vital to its interests. Although Peel had modified the sliding scale in 1842, he had resisted the demands of the Anti-Corn Law League for repeal. It is not surprising that his change of heart in 1846 shocked and split his party. However, the question of inconsistency depends on the angle from which the matter is examined. Undoubtedly Peel had gone against a long-established Tory policy and offended the landowning interest. Repeal of the Corn Laws was, however, consistent with the economic policies Peel had pursued since he came to power in 1841. It followed on from his free-trade budgets. Indeed, in many ways it was the logical consequence of the policies he had pursued since 1841 to tackle the 'condition of England' question – in his own words, 'to make this country a cheap country for living'. Professor Gash argues that it was this, not the Irish famine, which was the real reason for his 'conversion' to repeal.

Examiner's tip   Reference to leading historians will gain you credit provided it is brief, to the point and appropriately woven into your own argument.

This provides a clue to the underlying consistency of Peel's career. His major concern was the national interest. It was this that led him to give such importance to the 'condition of England' question. He regarded himself first and foremost as a minister of the crown rather than the leader of a party. The national interest also meant a concern for law and order and political stability, manifested in his penal reforms in the 1820s, his reluctant acceptance of Catholic emancipation in 1829 and his firm handling of Chartism in 1842. This same concern for political stability was also a factor in his conversion to repeal of the Corn Laws, for he was increasingly concerned that they were alienating the middle class from the political system. The fundamental political problem of his lifetime was the integration of the commercial and industrial middle classes into a political system dominated by the aristocracy. This, according to Professor Gash, was his lifework and it is this which provides the thread of consistency.

Viewed as a party leader, then, it is fair to charge Peel with inconsistency. For his critics in the Tory/Conservative Party his personality – cold and haughty – only made matters worse. But taken on his own terms as a minister of the crown intent on the national interest, this inconsistency may be better described as flexibility and pragmatism. As he himself said in 1846, he was overthrown because he put the interests of the nation before those of the party.

Examiner's tip The above answer is of Grade A standard because: (a) the answer focuses throughout on the idea of consistency – you will see that it features in every paragraph; (b) it always balances arguments for and against the charge of inconsistency; and (c) it moves on from specific events (Catholic emancipation, the repeal of the Corn Laws) to underlying ideas (party interest v. national interest).

Question 3

Examiner's tip There are only 6 marks for part (a): ration your time carefully. In part (b) the key words are 'how serious'. A narrative of disturbances will not produce an adequate answer.

Examiner's answer plan

(a) The end of the war was one reason: demobilisation and the end of wartime contracts caused distress. Consider other causes of economic distress: the industrial revolution, the Corn Laws, tax changes. Refer also to radical leaders such as Hunt and Cobbett.

(b) Divide the disturbances into more and less serious. The Spa Fields Riots, the March of the Blanketeers and Peterloo were no real threat (e.g. Peterloo was an over-reaction to a peaceful meeting). The Pentrich Rising and the Cato Street conspiracy were genuinely revolutionary in intention, but what were their chances of success? Were the government's fears exaggerated? Was political disturbance caused more by economic distress than revolutionary ideas? What chance did uncoordinated radical movements have of overthrowing a repressive government?

Question 4

Examiner's tip The question is about the *consequences* of the Reform Act: avoid irrelevance about its causes or the manner of its passing. To assess the significance of the changes it brought about you must also consider what it did not change.

Examiner's answer plan

Explain the terms of the Act and the changes which resulted: enfranchisement of the middle classes, abolition of many rotten boroughs and increased representation for the industrial midlands and north. Point out that change was limited: bribery continued, there was no secret ballot, some rotten boroughs survived. The working class remained outside the franchise and the electorate was still very small. Next discuss what the Act preserved. The composition of the House of Commons changed little. Government was still dominated by the aristocracy and the powers of the Lords were little affected. Thus by a limited reform, admitting the middle class into partnership, the Act preserved the aristocratic domination of politics, at least for the time being. The abolition of many rotten boroughs did, however, reduce the political influence of the crown. The real significance of the Act was not so much what it changed or preserved as the precedent it set for future reform.

Question 5

Examiner's tip The key phrase is 'constructive reform'. The question excludes the Reform Act.

Examiner's answer plan
Set out the provisions of the five main reforms – the education grant, the abolition of slavery, the Factory Act, the Poor Law Amendment Act and the Municipal Corporations Act – and, most importantly, *comment* on each of them, assessing their limitations as well as what they achieved. For example, the education grant was only £20 000; the new Poor Law was cheaper but highly unpopular and arguably the wrong response to urban unemployment. Comment on the reforming achievements of the period as a whole, noting how little reform there was after 1835. The rise of Chartism was partly caused by working-class disappointment with the Whig reforms.

Question 6

> **Examiner's tip** The key words are 'how serious'. The focus should be on assessment rather than description.

Examiner's answer plan
Discuss the three main Chartist outbreaks. In each case consider the level of violence and the threats the Chartists made (e.g. Newport rising, Sacred Month, Plug Plot, extremist rhetoric – especially from O'Connor). Examine the government's response – e.g. General Napier at Newport, special constables in 1848 – which suggests it was alarmed. Then discuss the weaknesses of Chartism to assess how serious a threat it posed. The relationship between the three outbreaks and the economic cycle is suggestive.

---

2   FOREIGN AFFAIRS, 1815–65

Question 1

> **Examiner's tip** The key word is 'effective'. The Examiner will be looking for judgements supported by specific references. Do not attempt to describe foreign policy issues in detail: use them selectively as the basis for comment.

There was more continuity in foreign policy between Castlereagh and Canning than contemporaries recognised. Their aims were similar, though their methods differed. Both aimed to uphold Britain's interests as a trading nation and a naval power and to maintain a balance of power in Europe in order to preserve peace and stability. Both saw France and Russia as the major threats to that balance and to Britain's interests. On the issue of support for constitutionalist governments, however, contemporaries detected a difference in attitude, though it was probably not as great as they thought.

> **Examiner's tip** This introduction lays a good foundation for the argument by setting out what Britain's foreign policy interests were, thus providing criteria by which effectiveness can be judged.

In pursuing these aims both had a mixture of success and failure. Castlereagh's greatest successes came in his early years as Foreign Secretary. Between 1812 and 1815 he was responsible for building up and holding together the Fourth Coalition, which brought about the overthrow of Napoleon. He went on to play a leading role in the settlement of Europe at the Congress of Vienna. He secured for Britain a number of islands and ports valuable as naval bases or for trade: the Cape, Mauritius, Trinidad, Tobago, St Lucia, Malta and Heligoland. The treaty met his aim of a balance of power. France was not treated vindictively, but safeguards against future French aggression were built into the treaty by the union of Belgium and Holland, the strengthening of Prussia's position in western Germany and the enlargement of the kingdom of Piedmont. Russia's acquisition of the Grand Duchy of Warsaw was balanced by Prussian gains in Saxony.

Castlereagh was less successful in his later years. He sought after 1815 to protect Britain's interests by turning the Quadruple Alliance into the Congress System, which he saw as a means of preserving the balance of power. The first Congress, at Aix-la-Chapelle in 1818, was successful. Its main outcome was the removal of the Allied army of occupation from France and the admission of France to the Congress System. In the later congresses, however, Britain's interests increasingly diverged from those of the other powers. This difference had its origin in Castlereagh's refusal in 1815 to join the Holy Alliance which he dismissed as 'a piece of sublime mysticism and nonsense'. When liberal revolutions broke out in Spain, Portugal and Naples in 1820, the other Congress powers wished to intervene to suppress them as a threat to European peace, a view they set out in the Troppau Protocol. Castlereagh rejected this in the State Paper of 1820; he believed that it was against Britain's interests to become involved in a commitment to intervention in the internal affairs of other states and so he only sent an observer to the Congress of Laibach in 1821. Nevertheless he was unable to prevent the other powers sanctioning Austrian intervention in Naples and by the time of his death Britain was at odds with the other members of the Congress System.

Canning's chief successes in promoting Britain's foreign policy interests were in Portugal and Latin America. In Portugal, a British fleet and 4000 troops intervened decisively in favour of the constitutionalist claimant to the throne against an absolutist. The motive was not so much sympathy for the Portuguese liberals as the fact that the absolutist was backed by Spain, which was in turn an ally of France. Furthermore, Canning wished to protect Britain's long-established trading relations with Portugal. In South America, too, his main aims were to protect British trade and thwart Spain and France. He had been unable to prevent the other powers at the Congress of Verona agreeing to French intervention in Spain to restore the absolutist monarch, but he was determined that France should not go on to restore Spanish control over the South American colonies. He was successful in this, helped by the issue of the Monroe Doctrine in the USA. As he famously remarked, 'I called the New World into existence to redress the balance of the old'.

The Greek question proved more difficult. The essential dilemma was that British sympathy for the Greek cause cut across Britain's interest in maintaining the Turkish empire as a bulwark against Russian expansion in the Mediterranean. Canning tried to resolve this by working with Russia in support of Greece. When the Turks called in Ibrahim Pasha, Canning's response was to make an agreement with Russia, later joined by France, to intervene and set up a semi-independent state in Greece. At this point Canning died, so we cannot tell whether he would have been successful in dealing with the problems which then arose. All we can say is that he had handled the situation skilfully up to that point.

Unlike Castlereagh, Canning went out of his way to court public opinion, and this, together with his support for the constitutionalists in Portugal and the Greek independence movement, made him more popular and therefore more effective in the eyes of contemporaries. It can also be claimed that he showed more realism than Castlereagh in dissociating himself from the Congress System. By so doing he freed Britain to pursue its own interests through, for example, its intervention in Portugal and its recognition of the South American republics. These arguments support the view that Canning was more effective in pursuing Britain's foreign policy interests than Castlereagh. However, the overthrow of Napoleon and the Vienna settlement are powerful arguments in Castlereagh's favour. Moreover, the Congress System, though ultimately a failure, was a worthwhile attempt to secure long-term peace in Europe, which was greatly in Britain's interest. When he saw it was being diverted into purposes which were not in Britain's interest, Castlereagh protested and in doing so laid down, in the State Paper of 1820, the principle of non-intervention on which Canning acted. Nevertheless, if one has to choose, perhaps Canning was the more effective because he was right that, once Napoleon had been overthrown, Britain's interests did diverge from those of the continental great powers.

Examiner's tip This essay displays good knowledge relevantly used. Every major development in foreign affairs is mentioned but always as the basis for comment on effectiveness. The conclusion draws together the comparison well.

Question 2

Examiner's tip Do not try to explain everything in detail; there is not time. Refer briefly to the problems Palmerston faced, concentrating on his success in handling them. It is useful to start by outlining his aims, to enable you to assess effectiveness.

Viscount Palmerston dominated British foreign policy for over 30 years. He has the reputation of a 'John Bull' figure who was outspoken and high-handed in asserting British interests. He saw it as Britain's role to act as the arbiter of Europe in maintaining the balance of power and this led him to view France and Russia with suspicion as the greatest threats to that balance. He also sought to advance Britain's trading interests and maintain its naval supremacy. He was generally sympathetic to constitutional governments in Europe, but only if they did not threaten British interests.

Between 1830 and 1841 Palmerston faced problems in Belgium, the Near East and the Iberian peninsula. In Belgium his fear was that France would gain too much influence as a result of the Belgian revolt of 1830. It had long been an aim of British policy to ensure that Belgium did not fall under the control of a major naval power. Palmerston worked with Louis Philippe on this issue, making it plain that he was not prepared to see Belgium under the rule of a French king. Ultimately he secured an independent Belgium under the rule of Leopold of Saxe-Coburg and in 1839 Belgian neutrality was guaranteed by international treaty. In the Near East Britain's aim was to safeguard its trading routes, and especially the route to India, against Russian expansion into the Balkans at the expense of Turkey. The Mehemet Ali crisis, which Russia exploited to gain effective control over the Dardanelles, alarmed Palmerston. In 1841 he was able to undo the damage by the Straits Convention and at the same time he warded off the danger of increased French influence in the Eastern Mediterranean. In the Iberian peninsula, Palmerston succeeded in helping the constitutionalist rulers of Spain and Portugal to defeat their absolutist rivals and also prevented France from gaining undue influence in the area by negotiating the Quadruple Alliance of Britain, France, Spain and Portugal.

In his handling of these three problems, Palmerston had furthered Britain's interests in several ways. All three areas were vital to Britain's naval strategy and trade. In all three cases he could claim that he had preserved the balance of power by averting threats from France and Russia. He had asserted Britain's influence in European affairs, for which he was not popular with European rulers and statesmen, but was applauded at home. Public opinion also approved of his support for constitutionalist rulers against absolutism in Spain and Portugal. Between 1830 and 1841, then, Palmerston was highly effective in promoting Britain's interests in Europe and the Near East. Furthermore, in 1839 he embarked on the Chinese Opium War, in which British naval power forced China to open some of its ports to British trade.

> **Examiner's tip**   Note how the survey of the main policies of 1830–41 is followed by a paragraph summing up his achievements.

After 1846 Palmerston continued to seek to maintain the balance of power and to view France and Russia as the main threats to it. He was not responsible for handling the main crisis in relations with Russia in this period, but as Prime Minister when the Crimean War ended he negotiated a peace treaty which asserted Turkey's independence and rejected Russia's claims in the Balkans. France he always regarded with suspicion. He fell out with Louis Philippe over the Spanish marriages, but approved of Louis Napoleon's coup d'état in 1851, seeing him as a force for stability in France. However in the period following the war of 1859 in Italy he saw Napoleon III's France as the greatest threat to the balance of power and in the early 1860s there was serious alarm about the possibility of war.

He also saw the 1848 revolutions as a threat to the balance of power. He regarded Austria as a force for stability in central Europe and made no protest at the suppression of the Hungarian rebels. At the same time his sympathy for liberalism pointed in the opposite direction – towards support for revolutionaries, as shown in his reaction to the visits of Haynau and Kossuth to London in 1849. His attitude to these won him popularity and angered the queen, but it is hard to see that in either case any important British interest was advanced. This is also true of the Don Pacifico affair, in which he again won public approval and royal disapproval for an action which in Europe was regarded as outrageous bullying.

Palmerston was able to throw his weight about in the Don Pacifico affair because of Britain's naval power. This is also true of the Second Chinese War (1856–60), which, like the first, was provoked by British aggression with the aim of increasing trade. Then in 1859 the British navy was instrumental in the success of Garibaldi's campaign to bring Naples and Sicily into the newly unified Italy.

Thus in the period from 1846 to about 1860, Palmerston was still effective in upholding British interests. His unpopularity with his European contemporaries indicates that he made Britain a force to be reckoned with. In comparing this period with 1830–41, however, it is fair to point out that no issue arose which affected Britain's vital interests quite so much as the Belgian or Mehemet Ali episodes (except the Crimean War, for which Palmerston was not responsible). It is in the early 1860s that Palmerston's foreign policy can justly be described as less effective. He was only rescued from a needless war against the northern states in the American Civil War by the good offices of Prince Albert. He blustered to no effect about the Russian suppression of the Polish Revolt in 1863. Most seriously, he was blind to the threat to the balance of power posed by Prussia and was outmanoeuvred by Bismarck over the Schleswig-Holstein question.

When Palmerston died, the balance of power in Europe was already shifting in a way he did not realise. It is hardly surprising, therefore, that he lost his sureness of touch in the 1860s. The period 1830–41 was indeed the period of his greatest success, but a fairer judgement would differentiate between the period 1846–51 and the early 1860s.

Examiner's tip The above answer is sensibly organised, with half the essay devoted to each of the two periods to be compared. It uses the evidence to reach a balanced, critical and well-supported view about the verdict suggested in the question. An alternative approach would be to organise the material under the headings such as defending British interests, upholding British prestige, maintaining the balance of power, support for nationalism and the promotion of trade. The two periods would then be compared under each heading (e.g. under the balance of power, relations with France in the 1830s over Belgium, the Near East, Spain and Portugal would be compared with the Spanish marriages issue and relations with Napoleon III in the later period).

Question 3

Examiner's tip The key phrase is 'most important principles'. Narrative on its own will not earn much credit. The dates mean Castlereagh and Canning (plus 1827–30), and the focus of the question is on continuity. Do not ignore 1812–15.

Examiner's answer plan

- Protecting Britain's trading interests – shown in the Vienna settlement, intervention in Portugal and recognition of the South American republics.

- The balance of power – shown in the struggle against Napoleon (Fourth Coalition), and the Vienna settlement. This principle led to suspicion of France (over its intervention in Spain and the former Spanish colonies) and of Russia (over the Holy Alliance and possible exploitation of the Greek revolt).

- Congress diplomacy (Castlereagh only).

- Non-intervention in smaller states' internal affairs – the State Paper of 1820, which laid down principles followed by Canning over Spain, Portugal and South America.

- Support for liberal governments – arguably a principle for Canning (e.g. in Portugal), though probably only when it was in Britain's interests.

Question 4

Examiner's tip The key word is 'considerations': it means more than 'principles' or 'aims'. The scope of the question is defined by the dates. A chronological approach is acceptable provided the emphasis is on analysis of the reasons for British policies rather than description.

Examiner's answer plan

The underlying 'consideration' was that British interests in the Eastern Mediterranean (trade, the route to India) required support for Turkey as a safeguard against Russian expansion. But there were other considerations which meant that this aim was pursued in different ways at different times. In the 1820s public sympathy for the Greek independence movement made it necessary to support the Greeks against the Turks and to cooperate with Russia. In the 1830s the main aim was to undo the Treaty of Unkiar Skelessi, but this was complicated by the threat to Turkey from Mehemet Ali and French support for Mehemet. In the 1850s Britain supported Turkey in a war against Russia resulting from Russian ambitions in the Near East.

3   GLADSTONE AND DISRAELI

Question 1

This is really a question about the reasons for the failure of Gladstone's attempts to solve the Irish problem. You are offered two explanations: make sure the Examiner sees how your material is related to them, and be prepared to offer other explanations as well.

It has been said that Gladstone failed in his 'mission to pacify Ireland' because he always did too little too late. Perhaps this is what is meant by describing English handling of the Irish problem between 1868 and 1894 as timid. In any case this is too sweeping a judgement on Gladstone's handling of the Irish problem, just as it is too simple to say that attempts to solve the problem were doomed by Irish extremism.

In his first ministry (1868–74), Gladstone believed that if he settled their grievances about the church and the land, the Irish would no longer demand repeal of the Union. He tackled these issues in the Disestablishment Act of 1869 and the First Land Act of 1870. With hindsight it is questionable whether he was correct in his belief that settling these two grievances would have solved the Irish problem, but in any case the Land Act was a failure. Irish tenants could still be evicted without compensation for non-payment of rent, unless the rent was 'exorbitant'. The House of Lords insisted on substituting this word for 'excessive', thereby making the provision worthless. The Act was not sufficiently radical in its approach to the land problem, but Gladstone could hardly have gone further in what many saw as an attack on property rights. To make matters worse, the onset of the agricultural depression in the mid-1870s led to a massive rise in the number of tenants unable to afford rents and thus in the number of evictions. There followed a wave of violence in rural Ireland, orchestrated by the Land League founded by Michael Davitt in 1879. It is doubtful whether this onset of Irish extremism could have been avoided even if the First Land Act had been less timid, since the root cause was the agricultural depression.

When Gladstone returned to power in 1880, therefore, the Irish situation had deteriorated. He still believed that the root of the problem was the land. The Second Land Act (1881) went much further than the first, offering Irish tenants the '3 Fs'. It certainly could not be called 'timid' except in its timing: it was ten years too late. It also failed to address the problem of rent arrears which had accumulated as a result of the depression, and it was therefore denounced by Parnell. Violence in Ireland was unabated and Gladstone had to resort to a Coercion Act in an attempt to restore order. An attempt to break out of the vicious circle of Irish violence and English coercion by the Kilmainham Treaty was wrecked by the most extreme act of terrorism of the period, the Phoenix Park murders. English opinion was outraged by this demonstration of Irish extremism.

Note that in the two preceding paragraphs the candidate explicitly relates the information to both Irish extremism and English timidity.

By 1855 Gladstone had become convinced that nothing short of Home Rule would bring peace to Ireland. Irish extremism played a part in the failure of his first Home Rule Bill in 1886: a substantial element of English public opinion regarded the Irish as unfit for self-government after the Phoenix Park murders. The primary reason for the failure, however, was the split in the Liberal Party with Chamberlain and Hartington leading 93 Liberal Unionists in voting against the Bill. No doubt they shared the widespread reaction against Irish extremism, but they had other motives. Chamberlain had personal reasons for turning against Gladstone and he believed that Home Rule for Ireland could be the first step in the break-up of the Empire. Another reason for opposing Home Rule which now became important was the question of Ulster, where the Protestant majority opposed Home Rule on religious grounds. Their cause was taken up by the Conservatives and Home Rule thus became a party issue. This accounts for the failure of Gladstone's second Home Rule Bill (1893) which was passed by the House of Commons after the Liberal victory in the election of 1892, but overwhelmingly defeated in the Conservative-dominated Lords.

Irish extremism, then, did play a part in the failure of efforts to solve the Irish problem. Paradoxically, however, it also advanced the Irish cause by underlining the strength of Irish support for Home Rule; this was a major factor in Gladstone's conversion to Home Rule. English timidity is also an inadequate explanation. Certainly, English attempts to solve the problem did not go far enough, but the reasons for this were complex and changed over time. Basically, the English did not understand what was needed in Ireland, and when they did recognise what the Irish wanted they were not willing to grant it. The land problem could have been solved earlier if there had been greater willingness to interfere with the rights of property. But it is questionable whether this would have solved the Irish problem. Probably only Home Rule could have provided a solution, but the English were unwilling to agree to it. The reasons for this had little to do with timidity and much more to do with genuine divisions of opinion and changing political circumstances. It is uncertain whether moderation on the Irish side would have helped either. The judgement offered oversimplifies a complicated historical problem.

> **Examiner's tip** This answer combines a survey of all the main aspects of Gladstone's attempts to solve the Irish problem with continuous attention to the reasons for his failure. The explanations suggested in the question are never forgotten, but they are also challenged and placed alongside other explanations offered by the candidate. This combination of strengths makes this an A Grade answer.

Question 2

> **Examiner's tip** This question is really about differences of principle and it covers all aspects of policy – domestic, foreign and imperial. Note also the word 'significant', which indicates that it is important to make some judgements.

It goes without saying that Gladstone and Disraeli were rivals for power. As leaders of their parties they fought three successive general elections. There was a deep personal antagonism between them, reflecting their very different personalities. But there were also significant differences of principle, as well as some underlying similarities of outlook which probably neither would willingly have acknowledged.

> **Examiner's tip** This brief introduction sets out the line the essay will adopt. Introductions need not be any longer if they are to the point.

In domestic affairs both Gladstone and Disraeli headed reforming ministries. In this sense there was little difference between them. But the philosophy underpinning their domestic policies was different and so was the emphasis of their reforms. 'Gladstonian liberalism' stemmed from Gladstone's commitment to individualism. It advocated civil and religious liberty, a minimal state, free trade, low taxes and equality of opportunity. Thus in his ministry of 1868–74, many of Gladstone's reforms were directed towards removing privileges and creating conditions in which individualism could flourish. Privileges were removed in the civil service, the army and the universities. A basic level of universal education was established by the Forster Act. Political liberty was enhanced by the Secret Ballot Act. Trade unions were given legal status but freedom of the individual worker from union pressure was safeguarded by making picketing illegal. All this added up to a considerable volume of reform, but it was administrative and legal rather than social reform. Indeed, it was not Gladstone's wish to change society, as was shown by his lack of interest in Chamberlain's radical reform programme in the 1880s.

Disraeli's political philosophy is known as 'Tory democracy'. Disraeli was not a rigorous political thinker and Tory democracy (a term not used by Disraeli himself) is not very easy to pin down. In essence, it amounts to a belief in an aristocratic, paternalist government protecting the poor through social reforms in an attempt to bring together the 'two nations' that Disraeli had identified in his early writing. As set out in his Crystal Palace speech, it was intended to win the support of the recently enfranchised working class for the Conservatives. It was also an attack on the individualism of Gladstonian liberalism, which Disraeli accused of endangering all the institutions of the country. In practical terms this led to much more social reform than in Gladstone's first ministry. The list in 1875–6 included the Public Health Act, the Artisans' Dwellings Act, the Sale of Food and Drugs Act, the Merchant Shipping Act, the Employers and Workmen Act and an Education Act. Disraeli also reversed the Gladstonian Act forbidding peaceful picketing, an interesting indication that he placed less emphasis on the rights of the individual.

In practice, however, the difference between the two in domestic reform was smaller than a description of their political philosophies would suggest. Although they were both involved in the extension of the franchise in the 1867 Reform Act, and both sought to win the new electorate for their parties, neither was truly a democrat in the modern sense. They accepted the basic class framework of Victorian society. It was Gladstone, not Disraeli, who said, 'I am a firm believer in the aristocratic principle'. And although Disraeli's ministry achieved more social reform, it was Cross rather than Disraeli who was responsible, and in any case the impact was much reduced by the permissive nature of much of the legislation. Perhaps the biggest difference between them in domestic affairs was over Ireland: Disraeli had little sympathy for the Irish whereas Gladstone's desire, based on his religious convictions, to secure fair treatment for them became almost an obsession.

| Examiner's tip | This discussion of political philosophy and its practical outcome in domestic affairs is promising. It sets out the main differences and assesses their significance. |

We must also consider whether there were important differences of principle on foreign and imperial affairs. Disraeli's Crystal Palace speech placed great emphasis on patriotism and pride in the Empire, and these became hallmarks of Disraelian conservatism. There was a clear difference of outlook between the two men on foreign policy. Gladstone based his policy on his strong moral sense, and so along with retrenchment and reform, Gladstonian liberalism stood for peace. This explains Gladstone's controversial decision to pay compensation to the USA for the Alabama affair, for which Disraeli attacked him. Hence, too, his outrage over the Bulgarian atrocities. His campaign on this was regarded by Disraeli as undermining Britain's true interest, which was to prevent Russia exploiting the situation. Gladstone's moral indignation was again directed against Disraeli in the

Midlothian campaign in 1879, this time against his imperial policies which led to the Zulu and Afghan Wars. Since imperialism was one of the key features of the Crystal Palace speech, it would seem that here too there was an important difference of principle between the two men. In practice, however, the differences were smaller. Disraeli's 'forward' policy in Afghanistan and South Africa, over which Gladstone attacked him, was as much the work of the men on the spot as of Disraeli himself. And, for all the vehemence of his attacks on Disraeli's imperialism, Gladstone's behaviour in Egypt was little different from what Disraeli would have done, except perhaps that Disraeli would have made more effort to rescue Gordon.

Thus there do seem to be real differences of principle between the two men. Gladstone's emphasis on individualism, self-help and the role of morality in politics were alien to Disraeli. Some would argue that Disraeli had no real principles and that his sole aim in politics was to reach the 'top of the greasy pole'. Even if this is so Gladstone was undoubtedly motivated by political principles and Disraeli's opposition to them was in itself a difference of principle.

Examiner's tip This answer is clearly structured and covers a lot of ground. Factual evidence is used selectively to underpin the argument rather than for description. Similarities are referred to as well as differences.

Question 3

Examiner's tip This question requires a well-organised and intelligent selection of ideas with factual detail used to support them. Avoid a narrative approach. It is probably best to divide the essay into sections on assets and liabilities.

Examiner's answer plan

- Assets: personality and energy; powers of oratory (Midlothian campaign); ability to appeal to the people (the People's William); strong moral dimension to politics (or was this a liability?); created the Liberal Party.
- Liabilities: obsession with Ireland, leading to split of party in 1886; lack of interest in social reform; inability to get on with Chamberlain; Gordon episode.

Question 4

Examiner's tip The key words are 'how and why'. 'How' is fairly straightforward – the split over Home Rule. 'Why' needs to be approached from a number of directions.

Examiner's answer plan

Explain the events of 1885–6, leading up to Chamberlain voting against Home Rule. Then discuss why he opposed it: fear of the break-up of the Empire, belief that the Irish were not fit for self-government and concern about the Ulster problem. Further sections should be devoted to personal relations between Gladstone and Chamberlain and to their differences over social reform. Chamberlain saw Gladstone, with his obsession with Ireland, as an obstacle to radical reform – hence the 'Unauthorised Programme' of 1885. Tactical considerations need discussion: Chamberlain hoped to return to the Liberal Party as its leader on Gladstone's retirement, which he thought could not be long delayed. Finally consider the underlying problem of the nature of the Gladstonian Liberal Party. Was it a radical party or not? It would seem that tensions over social reform strained it – Home Rule blew it apart.

Question 5

Examiner's tip   It is important to begin by defining 'Tory democracy'. Note that the question includes the period 1865–8.

Examiner's answer plan

Tory democracy was a paternalistic philosophy appealing to working-class sentiment through social reform and based on the idea of the 'two nations'. You should relate this to Disraeli's policies. In 1865–8 he deliberately set out to win the support of the respectable working class for the Conservatives by the Second Reform Act. Most of the material comes from 1874–80. The social reforms should be detailed and assessed. Note that they were permissive and in any case mainly the work of Cross. Disraeli himself seemed much more interested in foreign affairs and the 'forward' imperial policy; but in his Crystal Palace speech, in which he set out the ideas of Tory democracy (not a phrase he himself used), Disraeli linked it with patriotism and pride in the Empire.

4   THE EDWARDIAN AGE, 1901–14

Question 1

Examiner's tip   Be sure to address all aspects of this question. It involves both parties and requires you to understand what particular economic and social reforms the Examiner has in mind and how the parties might be thought to gain political advantage from them.

Social and economic issues played an important part in the politics of the Edwardian age. One of the major issues in the 1906 general election was tariff reform, which was advocated by Joseph Chamberlain. The Liberals who won that election then embarked on an extensive programme of social reform which has sometimes been regarded as the origin of the welfare state. What motives lay behind the adoption of these policies?

Examiner's tip   The candidate has used the introduction sensibly to set out an interpretation of the question and indicate which social and economic issues are most relevant.

Chamberlain came out in favour of tariff reform and imperial preference in 1903. With his Birmingham background, he was well aware of the economic problems facing Britain in the late nineteenth and early twentieth centuries as other countries, especially Germany and the USA, challenged its industrial might. He was aware, too, that they were building up their industry with the help of protective tariffs. He saw the answer to these problems in the Empire and this was the reason for his surprising decision to go to the Colonial Office in 1895. Tariff reform was a logical development of his imperialist ideas. Combined with a scheme of imperial preference it would protect British industry against foreign competition and would unite the Empire as an economic unit and in the long term politically as well. Thus there was a strong economic case for tariff reform.

There was, however, a political side to it as well. Chamberlain proposed to use the revenue raised by tariffs to fund social reforms, including an old age pension scheme such as Bismarck had set up in Germany. This would, he hoped, have the appeal to sell tariff reform to the electorate. In this he miscalculated. The main political results were to split the Unionist Party and to provide the Liberals with an election-winning issue (the big loaf v. the small loaf) around which they could unite. Tariff reform was probably the main reason for the overwhelming defeat of the Unionists in 1906. If the aim of tariff reform was to gain political advantage it backfired, but to say that Chamberlain advocated it purely for that reason would be to misjudge him.

Examiner's tip   These two paragraphs have explained the non-political and political reasons for the tariff reform campaign and struck a balance. This is promising.

There was also a mixture of motives behind the social reforms of the Liberal governments of 1905–14. Partly they arose from a conviction that social reform was urgently needed. The case for it had been amply documented by the work of Charles Booth and Seebohm Rowntree, both of whom had demonstrated that around one-third of the urban population was living below the poverty line. The failure of the Unionists to address this had been one, though not the most important, reason for their defeat in the 1906 election. The Liberals themselves were not united about social reform. One wing of the party, with a political pedigree derived from Gladstonian liberalism, was reluctant to increase state intervention. There were, however, powerful figures, notably Lloyd George and Churchill, who were strong advocates of social reform. These New Liberals, as they were called, had their roots in the radical wing of the Gladstonian Liberal Party which had produced Chamberlain's unauthorised programme in 1885. Through their efforts a great deal was achieved: school meals for needy children, school medical inspections, old age pensions, employment exchanges, the Trade Boards Act and finally the National Insurance scheme. In the process the challenge of the House of Lords, which threatened the Liberals' plans for financing these reforms, was overcome.

Examiner's tip   Note that the social reforms are not described in detail: the question is about the reasons for interest in social reform, not the reforms themselves.

Clearly there was political advantage to be gained from this. It gained support for the Liberals from working-class voters and, importantly, enabled them to outflank the challenge from the Labour Party, which had gained 29 seats in 1906. There was undoubtedly concern that the Labour Party would gain ground at the expense of the Liberals if they did not satisfy working-class demands for social reform. The 1910 elections showed that the Liberals had succeeded in maintaining working-class support against the challenge from Labour. Nevertheless it is doubtful whether fear of Labour was the main motive behind Liberal social reforms. This alleged fear has probably been exaggerated with hindsight in view of the collapse of the Liberals in the 1920s. Nor were their social reforms simply a bid for electoral success. Social reform was not the main feature of their campaign either in 1906, when the most important issue was tariff reform, or in 1910, when it was the House of Lords.

The truth is that in pushing through their social reforms the Liberals had mixed motives. Of course they hoped they would win support for them; that, after all, is what politics is about. But the New Liberals genuinely believed in social reform: that is what they were in politics for. In this sense, their reasons for advocating social reform were comparable to Chamberlain's in advocating protection – a mixture of policy objectives which they believed to be in the national interest and of seeking political advantage and electoral success in order to be able to carry out these policies.

> **Examiner's tip** In this answer political advantage is balanced against other motives for advocating reform. The answer focuses consistently on the motives for advocating reform.

Question 2

> **Examiner's tip** Part (a) is worth only 4 marks and therefore requires a relatively short answer.

(a) The main problem was that a number of organisations had arisen with different ideas about aims and methods. There were differences both between and within the socialist societies and the trade unions. The two main socialist societies were the SDF which was Marxist and revolutionary, and the Fabian Society, which advocated piecemeal reform. There were also different views in the trade unions. The leaders of the 'new unions' of unskilled workers were more interested in using political means to improve the conditions for their members than the leaders of the craft unions. Many of the latter were satisfied with the existing Lib-Lab arrangements which had brought a handful of working men into Parliament since the 1870s and were not interested in setting up a separate party. This explains why Keir Hardie found it so difficult to win union support for the Independent Labour Party which he founded in 1893. Another problem was that both the Liberal and the Conservative Parties had their working-class wings and so any attempt to set up a separate Labour group would face competition for working-class voters from well-organised and well-financed parties. It would also have to create its own national organisation from scratch with limited finances.

(b) The main aim of the newly formed Labour Representation Committee in 1900 was to establish a separate Labour group in the House of Commons. Why did the unions and the socialist societies want such a group? For the trade unions the main purpose was to use Parliament to strengthen the position of the unions. They also saw in it a way of advancing the fundamental purpose for which they existed – to improve living and working conditions and wages for their members. In other words the underlying aim was to use parliamentary representation to achieve social change by laws to strengthen workers' rights (e.g. in wage bargaining) and to provide for social welfare. For the socialists, a Labour group in Parliament was a way to achieve their fundamental belief in a reordering of society to bring justice to the working classes, and particularly to eradicate the poverty revealed by Booth's survey of the London poor. This would mean state-provided welfare (pensions, health and unemployment insurance) and redistributive taxation. Thus for both groups social change was ultimately the main aim. Strengthening the position of the unions and securing a Labour group in Parliament were important but subordinate.

> **Examiner's tip** This answer for part (b) covers the aims of both the unions and the socialist organisations, sets them out systematically and relates them explicitly to social change.

(c) The LRC faced its first general election within months in October 1900, and was able to secure the election of only two MPs. In its first few years, therefore, what influence it was able to exert on the other two parties was outside Parliament.

The Conservatives who were in power until the end of 1905 did little that pleased Labour and much that offended it. The Unemployed Workmen Act of 1905, a limited step towards helping the unemployed, and the Education Act of 1902, an important step forward in state education, both benefited the working classes, though Nonconformists, who were to be found among supporters of Labour as well as the Liberals, were offended by the Education Act's support for church schools. Labour, like the Liberals, opposed tariff reform on the grounds that it would lead to dearer food. Labour supporters were outraged by the Conservative government's approval of the Chinese labour scheme in South Africa. Worst of all was the Conservatives' reaction to the Taff Vale judgement, which threatened to make it impossible for trade unions to call a strike. The most Balfour was willing to do was to set up a Royal Commission. Thus the Conservatives took very little notice of Labour views.

The Liberals were more sympathetic to Labour views. For 30 years there had been working-class Liberals in Parliament (the Lib-Labs) and the radical wing of the Liberal Party, led by Lloyd George and Churchill, supported a programme of social reform which had much in common with that of the Labour Party. In 1906 only a beginning could be made with this programme, but a first instalment of welfare provision, the School Meals Act, was passed; this was a Labour initiative which was accepted by the Liberal government. Also in 1906 the Liberals reversed the Taff Vale judgement by the Trade Disputes Act, the final version of which closely reflected trade union views. It seems, therefore, that Labour had rather more influence on the Liberals than on the Conservatives, but one would need to examine the whole of the work of the Liberal ministry, which is beyond the scope of this question, to decide how much influence they had.

The real importance of the years 1900–6 for the Labour Party, however, lies not in its influence (or lack of it) on the two major parties but in its success in establishing itself. The Taff Vale judgement was a turning point for Labour because it convinced the trade union movement, which at first was rather lukewarm in its support of the LRC, that parliamentary representation was vital to secure the reversal of the judgement. The LRC began to win seats in local elections and by-elections. In the 1906 general election, it won 29 seats and along with the Lib-Labs formed a Labour group of over 50 MPs. This was achieved partly as a result of an electoral pact with the Liberals, but also because of the success of the LRC in winning support from the trade union movement.

By 1906, then, the infant Labour Party had had only limited success in influencing the two major parties, but it had succeeded in its inital objective of establishing a distinct Labour group in Parliament. Whether it would ever be more than a ginger group on the left of the Liberals remained to be seen.

| **Examiner's tip** | The structure of this answer for part (c) follows closely the wording of the question, thus ensuring the relevance which Examiners look for. Note too that in each section there is an explicit judgement about Labour's success. This level of effectively sustained judgement makes this a Grade A answer. |

Question 3

Examiner's tip The key phrase is 'Tory divisions and mistakes'. It is probably best to discuss the two parties in turn, as the quotation suggests.

Examiner's answer plan

- Weaknesses of the Conservatives. Division over tariff reform. Unpopularity with certain sectors of the electorate – 1902 Education Act; 1904 Licensing Act; 1901 Taff Vale judgement. Chinese labour scandal. Failure to tackle social problems.
- But there was a positive side to the Liberal victory: tariff reform had reunited a party divided on imperialism, the Boer War and the extent to which the state should intervene in social and economic affairs. The Liberals also benefited from an electoral pact with the Labour Representation Committee.

Question 4

Examiner's tip To answer this well you will need to decide what you think makes a constitutional crisis. There is no 'correct' definition. You will need a good knowledge of the issues involved and the development of events.

Examiner's answer plan

Explain the background to the crisis – the 1906 election result and the rejection of Liberal Bills by the Conservative House of Lords in 1906–8. Then go on to the 1909 budget, the reasons why the Lords rejected it and the development of events through 1910–11, culminating in the passage of the Parliament Act. Undoubtedly it was at least a serious quarrel between the parties: the Conservative House of Lords was in conflict with a Liberal ministry which had a majority in the Commons. The *issue* involved was a constitutional one: the powers of the hereditary House of Lords in a democracy. But the quarrel was resolved in a constitutional manner. Two general elections demonstrated the support of the electorate for the Parliament Act and in the end the Lords accepted it, despite the opposition of the 'Die-hards'. The king was not required to honour his pledge to create new peers to carry it. The conclusion is that in the end neither party quite pushed it to the extent of a constitutional *crisis*.

5   BRITAIN, EUROPE AND THE EMPIRE, 1885–1914

Question 1

Examiner's tip The key words are 'drifted' and 'unnecessary'. Make sure you reach a conclusion on their validity.

As the crisis of July/August 1914 developed, it was by no means certain that Britain would enter the war. There were long debates in the Cabinet as to what its commitments were and where its interests lay. To understand why there was such uncertainty we need to examine the development of Britain's relations with France, Russia and Germany from the turn of the century.

In 1900 Britain had no allies and no commitments. The description of this isolation as 'splendid' was, however, coming increasingly into question. The other Great Powers were linked in two opposing alliances: the Triple Alliance of Germany, Austria-Hungary and Italy, and the Dual Alliance of France and Russia. Britain had long-standing colonial differences with France and Russia, and then, in the late 1890s, tension developed between Britain and Germany. The two main causes of this were the expansion of the German navy under Tirpitz's Navy Laws and pro-Boer attitudes in Germany during the Boer War.

In these circumstances British diplomacy began to seek allies. In 1902 an alliance was made with Japan. This was not a case of 'drift' but a response to the threat of Britain's interests in the Far East posed by Russia's invasion of Manchuria. Approaches were made to Germany for an alliance in 1898 and 1899, but were rebuffed. Britain turned to France, not for an alliance but for an agreement which would reduce the dangers of isolation by removing sources of tension. This was achieved by the Entente Cordiale of 1904, in which Egypt was recognised as a British sphere of influence and Morocco as a French one. It must be stressed that this entente involved no 'commitment': it was not comparable to the Triple or Dual Alliances. Nevertheless it began a period of increasing cooperation between Britain and France, largely stimulated by Germany's behaviour. This process began almost at once when Germany, seeking to drive a wedge between Britain and France, challenged French influence in Morocco and demanded an international conference on the matter. At the Algeciras Conference Britain supported French claims and the result was to strengthen the Entente rather than weaken it as Germany hoped. Moreover, because of Germany's threatening attitude, military talks were begun between Britain and France. This was still not an alliance, but it was something more than an entente – the beginning of a 'drift' into greater commitment.

In 1907 a further entente was signed with Russia. This was a logical step in view of the existence of an Anglo-French entente and a Franco-Russian alliance. Like the Entente Cordiale, it involved settling differences, in this case over Persia, Afghanistan and Tibet. Again it was not an alliance and involved no commitment to support Russia. Before long however, the inter-linked agreements between Britain, France and Russia began to be known as the Triple Entente, matching the Triple Alliance: Britain was gradually becoming more closely identified with one of the two camps into which pre-war Europe was divided.

In the period between 1907 and 1914 Britain tried to preserve good relations with Germany, but Germany's naval policy and its behaviour in the various international crises of these years, particularly the Agadir crisis of 1911, drove it closer to France. In the Agadir crisis, the prospect of a German naval base on the Atlantic coast of Morocco led to Lloyd George's Mansion House speech, in which he warned that Germany was risking war – a war in which Britain and France would have been on the same side. Germany backed down. Meanwhile British alarm at the growth of the German fleet led to an expanded Dreadnought programme and an agreement with France in 1912 that the British navy should have the primary responsibility for naval defence in the Channel and the Atlantic and France in the Mediterranean. Again it was stressed that this was not an alliance, but it undoubtedly increased the level of Britain's commitment to France.

Examiner's tip   So far, the essay has given a good account of the development of Britain's commitments from 1900. The Examiner is now looking for further discussion of the two key concepts in the question.

In 1914, then, Britain was still not an ally of France and Russia. On the other hand it could be argued that it was morally obliged to come to the aid of France. Was not France entitled to expect Britain to defend the Channel in the event of a Franco-German war? Although Britain had deliberately avoided full alliance, the agreements it had made were viewed by the French, with much justification, as tantamount to an alliance. However, it would be unfair to Grey, the Foreign Secretary, to say he had 'drifted' into this position. He had developed cooperation with France to safeguard Britain's defence interests but avoided commitments which would allow France or Russia to drag Britain into an unnecessary war.

Nevertheless these commitments did lead Britain into war in 1914. Had Grey allowed himself to be drawn into commitments which had the effect he had tried to avoid? It seems not. Britain was not dragged into a war which France had caused or could have prevented. Nor was it a war in French rather than British interests. It would not have been in Britain's interest to stand by and watch Germany defeat France: German domination of Europe would have destroyed the balance of power. For this reason, it would not have been an unnecessary war, even if Germany had not invaded Belgium. However, this act, which cut across Britain's long-standing interest in preventing a major naval power controlling the Belgian coastline, made it all the more necessary. It is sometimes suggested that Britain could have prevented the war by making a clearer commitment to France and Russia, because this would have prevented Germany's miscalculation that Britain would stay out of the war. But the evidence seems to show that Germany had taken possible British entry into the war into its calculations and had still not been deterred. Overall, therefore, the judgement cannot be sustained.

> **Examiner's tip** The last two paragraphs are directed to considering the nature of Britain's commitments and the discussion is firmly linked to the two key words in the question. The essay is critical in approach and shows awareness of differing views. These qualities make it a Grade A answer.

Question 2

> **Examiner's tip** The key is interpreting the quotation: hope and anxiety about what? You will also need to comment on the adjectives 'exaggerated' and 'over-heated'.

Examiner's answer plan

After an introduction referring to the 'scramble for Africa' and the debate on the motives for imperialism, consider economic motives (the 'hope' of the quotation): markets for British goods, sources of raw materials, possibility of settling emigrants. Probably these hopes were exaggerated. Only some parts of Africa were suitable for European settlement and not all offered useful raw materials or commodities. Was Africa potentially a good market for British goods? Go on to discuss rivalry with other European powers ('anxiety'): French ambitions in Egypt and Sudan, German colonies in East, West and South West Africa. 'Overheated'? Note that Africa was partitioned without conflict between European powers, though it came close at Fashoda. Refer to treaties of 1884–5 and 1890. The only important conflict was the Boer War which was different – not a conflict with another European power. There was also another motive, bringing 'civilisation' to Africa, though less important than the other two motives. Finally, point out that the same combination of motives was also at work in China, with Russia and Japan as additional elements in the rivalry.

Question 3

The focus should be on 'responsibility' for the Boer War – the Boers' responsibility as well as Britain's.

Examiner's answer plan

Explain how the war began – a Boer ultimatum, followed by attacks on Cape Colony. Discuss the background of hostility between the Boers and the British – the Great Trek – the First Boer War. The main part of the essay should be devoted to sections on the contribution of each side to the growing tension. Why did the Boers feel threatened by the ambitions of Rhodes? How important was the Jameson Raid? What part was played by Boer treatment of the Uitlanders and Kruger's ambition to create a United States of South Africa? Explain the events of 1898–9. Which side bore the greater responsibility for the break-down of the Kruger-Milner talks?

Question 4

Examiner's tip There are a number of key phrases: 'how far', 'direct result', 'growing threat'. You will need to discuss not only the reasons for the deterioration of Anglo-German relations but also other reasons for Britain's emergence from isolation.

Examiner's answer plan

Germany's emergence as a great commercial and industrial power and the development of its overseas empire created underlying tensions. The threat it posed was brought home through (a) its response to events in South Africa (the Jameson raid, the Boer War); (b) its naval programme; (c) the Berlin-Baghdad railway; (d) its unwillingness to make an alliance; and (e) the personality of Kaiser William II. This was at a time when the dangers of isolation were shown by the Fashoda incident and the hostility of most of Europe during the Boer War. Fear of Russia was also a powerful incentive to seek allies, leading to the Anglo-Japanese alliance of 1902. Meanwhile, relations with France were improving, leading to the Entente Cordiale. Germany's response to this actually strengthened the Entente (Algeciras Conference).

6 THE INTER-WAR YEARS

Question 1

Examiner's tip This is not just a question about the Conservative Party.

The Conservatives were in office either as the governing party or as the dominant party in a coalition for the whole of the inter-war period except for the brief interval of the two Labour ministries. Clearly this must in part be because of their popularity with the electors. For a full explanation of their domination, however, we must also consider the condition of the Labour and Liberal Parties at this time.

The electoral success of the Conservatives was in large measure due to the personality of Stanley Baldwin, their leader from 1923 to 1937. Baldwin's image of pipe-smoking unflappability was reassuring. His attraction was his apparent ordinariness, though he was in a reality a shrewd and skilful political tactician. True, on occasion the image he projected worked against the Conservatives, as in 1929 when his slogan, 'Safety First', failed to catch the mood of the country. But on the whole, and especially in times of crisis – the General Strike, the 1931 financial crisis, the abdication crisis – he was trusted. Under him the Conservative Party seemed a party of moderation, financial orthodoxy and administrative competence, all of which reassured the middle classes. It seems likely also that on the whole the Conservatives benefited from the extension of the vote to women.

Nevertheless, at least equally important in explaining the dominance of the Conservatives in this period was the weakness of their opponents. The elections of the 1920s were three-cornered contests, with the anti-Conservative vote split between Labour and the Liberals. The Liberals, divided by the quarrel between Lloyd George and Asquith in 1916, came third to Labour in the 1922 general election and never recovered, even though the split was healed in 1923. The decline of the Liberals benefited the Conservatives in two ways. Firstly, many former Liberals turned to the Conservatives in order to keep out Labour (though, of course, others moved over to Labour). Secondly, however, Liberal support remained strong enough through the 1920s to prevent Labour winning an overall majority in a general election.

Labour, too, had handicaps which worked to the Conservatives' advantage. In the 1920s it was a relatively new party, still establishing its claim to be the main alternative to the Conservatives. Its success in doing this was remarkable enough; in 1929 it emerged from the general election as the biggest single party, though without an overall majority. It had a solid base in the working classes and the backing of the trade unions, but this was a disadvantage as well as an advantage, for it frightened some Liberals who saw it as a class party. Moreover many voters distrusted it because of its socialist aims and because of its leaders' lack of experience of high office. To many voters Labour seemed a gamble, while Baldwin by contrast offered reassurance.

In the 1930s Labour suffered a new handicap as a result of the crisis of 1931. The 'betrayal' of MacDonald gave it the appearance of disunity, though in reality only a small minority of the party followed him. The collapse of the second Labour ministry in the face of the financial crisis convinced many that it was not fit for government. Labour then refused to join the National government in circumstances which a majority of electors thought required a coalition. The National government was therefore Conservative dominated and won an overwhelming majority for a 'doctor's mandate' in the 1931 election. Labour was almost wiped out, though it recovered somewhat in 1935.

> **Examiner's tip** Note the clear structure of the essay: after the introduction, there are paragraphs about the Conservatives, the Liberals, Labour in the 1920s and Labour after 1931 – and they all focus on analysis rather than description.

The 1931 election was the outstanding occasion in the period when political circumstances worked to the Conservatives' advantage. An examination of the elections of the 1920s also shows that circumstances favoured them (or were turned to their advantage). In 1922 they (and the Labour Party) profited from the split in the Liberals between Asquith and Lloyd George. The Conservatives lost the election of 1923 (one of the only two in the period which they did lose) because Baldwin fought it on a programme of protection. Even this 'mistake' on Baldwin's part, however, can be seen as contributing to the later strength of the Conservatives, as it united the Conservatives and distanced them from their Liberal partners in the post-war coalition; in this way it laid the foundations for victory in the 1924 election. In this election, MacDonald's reopening of relations with Russia, followed by the Zinoviev letter, helped Baldwin to a convincing victory which put the Conservatives in office for five years. Conservative gains were mainly from the Liberals, many of whom turned to the Conservatives to keep Labour out. In 1929 the Conservatives again lost their overall majority and a minority Labour government came in, only to be overtaken by the Great Depression. We have already noted how this in turn led to the victories of the Conservative-dominated National governments in 1931 and 1935.

Thus the transitional state of British politics in the 1920s, with the rise of Labour and the decline of the Liberals, explains the dominance of the Conservatives in the first half of the period under discussion, while in the 1930s they benefited from the political fall-out from the Great Depression. In retrospect we can see how lucky the Conservatives were to lose the 1929 election. Their financial orthodoxy and air of calm competence were what the electorate wanted in the 1930s. It was not until 1945 that the electors reacted against the failures of the Conservatives in the 1930s in both domestic and foreign policies.

Examiner's tip This answer displays the qualities of clear organisation, relevant use of an appropriate selection of evidence and a range of explanations. In addition, it demonstrates a grasp of the interaction of the various factors and draws them together to produce a fully developed explanation.

Question 2

Examiner's tip The key words are 'sensible and practical'. You will need to consider the arguments for and against appeasement and apply them to the main international problems of the 1930s. You will need to be selective.

After 1945 appeasement was universally blamed as a major cause of the Second World War and Baldwin and Chamberlain were reviled as the guilty men. Yet in the context of its time, there is a case to be made for it as a sensible and practical policy. It is unfair to blame Baldwin and Chamberlain for pursuing a policy which most of their fellow-countrymen agreed with. It was a popular policy. There was a strong wish to avoid a repetition of the horrors of the First World War, as shown in the East Fulham by-election and the Peace Ballot. Many people felt guilty about the harshness of the Versailles peace settlement and thought fairness to Germany required some revision of it. The politicians were also influenced by awareness of Britain's comparative military weakness and fear of the Soviet Union, against which Hitler's Germany could be a bulwark.

Examiner's tip This introduction tackles immediately the underlying case for regarding appeasement as 'sensible and practical'.

To people at the time these arguments were strong, but this does not mean that appeasement was the right policy to pursue. To determine whether it was sensible, it is necessary to examine Britain's responses to the aggressions of Mussolini and Hitler, beginning with those issues which arose in 1935–6: the invasion of Abyssinia, German rearmament and the reoccupation of the Rhineland.

There is a good case for the view that a firmer line should have been adopted over Abyssinia. The handling of the crisis sent out all the wrong signals, especially to Hitler. The failure to impose sanctions on oil and the Hoare-Laval Plan showed that Britain and France were not prepared to take effective action against Italy, which duly went on to complete the conquest of Abyssinia. Nevertheless, there is a case to be made for Britain's policy. It is not certain that sanctions on oil would have worked, but Mussolini did threaten war if they were imposed. Was public opinion really prepared for that? In any case, Britain was anxious not to push Italy into the arms of Hitler.

Hitler was, indeed, the greater worry. In 1935 he embarked on an open policy of rearmament. It was in response to this, and to his abortive attempt to establish Nazi control in Austria in 1934, that the Stresa Front was formed with France and Italy. This was why Britain tried to have it both ways over Abyssinia, condemning Italy but trying to avoid alienating it. In the event Abyssinia was not saved and Italy did become an ally of Germany: this is the real reason for saying that appeasement of Italy was not a sensible policy.

Hitler's next aggression was the reoccupation of the Rhineland in 1936. Again Britain took no action and again it is questionable whether this was the right policy. Baldwin acted as he did because he thought the risk of war was too great and Britain too unprepared. He was aware too that many people in Britain thought Hitler's action not unreasonable – Germany was only entering 'her own back garden'. But with hindsight it seems likely that he overestimated Germany's ability to resist and that this was the last point at which Hitler's aggression could have been checked. For this reason appeasement was probably not the most sensible policy at this point.

> **Examiner's tip** Note how each of the two preceding paragraphs ends with a judgement about whether the policy was sensible.

There was little Britain could do about the *Anschluss* in March 1938, even though it was a breach of the Treaty of Versailles. On this issue appeasement was the only sensible and practical policy. Much more controversial is Munich. Chamberlain's claim that he had achieved peace with honour was his justification for appeasement and he seems to have believed Hitler's claim that this was his last territorial demand. He was, of course, wrong, but at the time public opinion approved. He had no wish to get embroiled in war over an issue (the Sudetenland) which did not directly threaten British interests, and he was conscious that Britain was not prepared for war, particularly in its air defences. He also argued that there was little Britain could do to help Czechoslovakia ('a far away country'). For these reasons Chamberlain thought appeasement was both sensible and practical.

If the purpose of appeasement at Munich was to prevent war, however, it was not 'sensible and practical'. The conclusion Hitler drew was that Britain and France would in the end back down rather than risk war. His occupation of Prague in March 1939 proved that he was not a reasonable man with demands which could be satisfied by concessions. At this point Chamberlain moved away from appeasement and gave a guarantee to Poland, which eventually led to the outbreak of war in September 1939.

It is an oversimplification to draw a dividing line in 1936 and say that appeasement was sensible and practical before it but not after. It is true that resistance to aggression would have been sensible and could have been successful in 1936 when Hitler occupied the Rhineland. But the same could also be said of Abyssinia in 1935. On the other hand, in the crises of 1938 over the Anschluss and the Sudetenland, appeasement was perhaps the only sensible option available because of Germany's lead in rearmament and because it was hard to see how Britain could mount effective military action in Austria or Czechoslovakia. Moreover, it still seemed possible after Munich that appeasement would lead to a period of greater international stability. With hindsight we know that this hope was false. By March 1939 Chamberlain knew it was false, and appeasement then clearly ceased to be sensible and practical.

Examiner's tip The above answer does not try to cover every development but selects the most controversial ones so that it can concentrate on the crucial issue: was appeasement sensible and practical? The candidate understands that the view put forward in the question is for discussion, not necessarily acceptance, and therefore rejects it in the conclusion after consideration of the evidence.

Question 3

Examiner's tip The mark allocation suggests that you should spend longer on the first part. The quotation gives you a useful starting point for the first part.

Examiner's answer plan

(a) An outline of the events of 1925–6 in the coal industry, beginning with the demand by the owners for wage cuts and ending with their lockout of the miners on 1 May 1926 shows that both sides were inflexible. Discuss why the mining industry was in such trouble. Then examine other causes. The strike had its roots in the development of the trade union movement: its growth before 1920, its comparative decline with the onset of depression in 1921 and the influence of syndicalism. The TUC's attitude encouraged the miners; both the miners and the TUC were influenced by memories of Black Friday, 1921. The government's handling of the dispute played a part. Baldwin expected and prepared for a general strike and finally provoked it by breaking off negotiations.

(b) The government was prepared for the strike and ensured that services continued to run. Through the *British Gazette* it put over its case, portraying the strike as a challenge to the authority of Parliament. The TUC was less well prepared; its leaders became afraid that the strike would lead to violence, possibly revolution, and that they would lose control to extremists. They were also worried by the charge that the strike was illegal. They seized the opportunity to end the strike offered by the Samuel compromise.

Question 4

Examiner's tip The key words are 'successful' and 'creditable'. The question is about the record of the ministry as a whole, not just its reforms.

Examiner's answer plan

The introduction can refer to the problems faced when Baldwin came to power in 1924: economic depression, unemployment and industrial unrest. Discuss the ministry's record of reform: the Local Government Act of 1929, the improvement of old age pensions in 1925, the extension of the vote to women aged 21–30 in 1928, the Trade Disputes Act and the establishment of the BBC. Was this a 'creditable record'? Then consider other aspects. The most important are the handling of the General Strike, the return to the gold standard and the unemployment problem. Foreign policy (Locarno) can also be mentioned. The verdict of the electors in 1929 is suggestive.

Question 5

The key word is 'betrayed'. You will need to argue a case for and against describing MacDonald's conduct in this way.

Examiner's answer plan

Begin by outlining the events of 1931. Outline the case against MacDonald: he failed to consult his colleagues who were shocked and regarded his behaviour as due to love of office. Their bitterness was compounded by the disastrous 1931 election result. Then go on to the case for MacDonald. The crisis was serious: there was a run on sterling and the underlying problem of the Great Depression. A coalition was an appropriate response. Explain the role of the king and Baldwin in persuading MacDonald. Next consider the effects on the Labour Party, which was reduced to 52 MPs in the 1931 election and was out of office until 1945. But you should question whether he 'undid all that he had achieved' – Labour's strength (6.5 million votes) was greater than the 1931 election result suggested and it recovered. Anyway, the disaster was as much the fault of the Labour Party itself, which had run away from the crisis. The verdict that MacDonald betrayed his party is political mythology.

Question 6

The key words are 'how successfully'. To reach a judgement on this you need to explain what the problems were and how they were tackled.

Examiner's answer plan

The underlying problems were the decline of the older staple industries and the consequent decline in exports and rise in structural employment. On top of these there were problems of adjustment to the economic effects of the First World War and then the Great Depression. The main government policies were insistence on a balanced budget, expenditure cuts (the Geddes Axe, the May Committee), protection (rejected in 1923 but introduced in 1932), the return to and subsequent abandonment of the gold standard and the Special Areas Act. Each of these should be assessed and the alternative policies advocated by Keynes should be considered. For an overall judgement, note that the level of unemployment remained high throughout the period and the problem of the depressed areas was not solved. On the other hand, there was a rise in the general standard of living, and many areas prospered in the later 1930s.

7 INTERNATIONAL DIPLOMACY, 1815–56

Question 1

The key words in this question are 'cynical ... self-interest' and 'considered ... balance of power'. You must explain what these meant in the early nineteenth century. You must be able to apply the terms of the Congress of Vienna to the question. 'More accurate view' means that you must discuss both interpretations and you should make your preference clear.

The most immediate intention of the Congress of Vienna was to settle Europe after the defeat of Napoleon. He had brought war to Europe for 15 years and, before him, the French Revolution had threatened the ruling classes of Europe. In a sense, both statements are true. Self-interest led the victorious powers to seek a stable peace after the conflict and a balance of power was needed to ensure that no country could again endanger security. Napoleon's 'Hundred Days' were a brief threat but did not seriously affect the settlement.

Examiner's tip	This is a good introduction. Very relevant, it focuses immediately on the key words and opens lines of argument which will be developed later. The background to 1814 is brief; the answer avoids unnecessary narrative.

The leaders of the most powerful countries met at Vienna. Metternich, Chancellor of Austria, was the host and probably the most influential statesman at the meeting. Castlereagh was present as British Foreign Secretary. Hardenberg represented Prussia. Alexander I of Russia was the only monarch to attend. Other countries, including small states, were represented but they did not influence the decisions which were made. It may seem unusual that Talleyrand attended because France was the aggressor but he persuaded the other statesmen that his presence would help to restore peaceful relations. A very clever politician, Talleyrand was successful in limiting the punishment of France.

National self-interest was paramount. Although they were eager to come to an agreement, the victorious statesmen were determined to defend their countries' interests. They had cooperated against Napoleon's wars but their alliance had not been close and they had different aims. Napoleon's wars had harmed every country in Europe and it seemed reasonable in the interests of the victors to punish France. Another aspect of self-interest was the wish to maintain the peace. The statesmen wanted to ensure that war would not break out again.

These motives were not cynical. It may have been harsh to decide the terms of the settlement without consulting fully the small states but it is unrealistic to think that these minor powers could have changed any of the decisions which were made. With hindsight, some of the decisions may seem wrong but they appeared to be fair at the time. There were protests later and nationalists sought to change the arrangements agreed at Vienna but, in 1815, it seemed as if the settlement was successful in solving the main problems left by Napoleon.

There was no real contradiction between self-interest and the balance of power. In peacetime, the rivalry between the major countries became apparent. For example, Russia had ambitions in eastern Europe, especially Poland, and Prussia sought to extend its influence over the smaller German states such as Saxony. These issues could cause trouble with Austria which wanted to maintain its role in central Europe and its pre-eminence over Germany. The statesmen compromised so that no country could threaten another and no major country was completely dissatisfied. The balance of power was more important than individual self-interest which might threaten peace.

Balance also involved security against France. Louis XVI was restored as king. In the eyes of other monarchs, he was the rightful ruler of France and his restoration was intended to erase the memory of the Revolution and Napoleon. Conquered territories were taken away and a protective barrier of states was constructed around France. Talleyrand managed to persuade the conquerors that his country had changed and that it was preferable to welcome its cooperation. This contrasts with the treatment of Germany after the First World War. Although France was punished further after the 'Hundred Days', the punishment was not severe. It lost more territories, had to pay reparations and also had to suffer an army of occupation.

The essay has developed well. It concentrates on the argument, explaining 'self-interest' and 'balance', and has avoided low-level description, but applies the key words to particular developments. The comparison with Germany after the First World War shows how a very good point can be made briefly.

The terms of the settlement affected every region of Europe. The Austrian Netherlands became part of Holland as a buffer against France. This represented both self-interest and the balance of power. Prussia became the most important state in the new German Confederation and gained the Rhineland. Austria was compensated for the loss of the Netherlands by the acquisition of Lombardy and Venetia in Italy. Therefore it maintained its self-interest by gaining territories to replace those which it lost and this contributed to the balance of power. Legitimate monarchs were restored to power in Spain and in Italian states. Although they were despots, their restoration seemed justified in 1815 because they had been deprived of their power by Napoleon. The Pope, who had been humiliated by Napoleon, regained Rome. In addition, the Congress decided to reorganise the Scandinavian countries. Denmark had supported Napoleon and lost Norway to Sweden. In turn, Russia received Finland from Sweden and controlled Poland. Britain's self-interests were satisfied by gains overseas such as Malta, the Cape of Good Hope, Cyprus and islands in the West Indies.

Examiner's tip This is a highly factual paragraph but the facts are used to sustain an argument. The facts without argument would be worth a lower mark.

The changes were largely successful. Peace was restored and, while there were nationalist risings in Italy, Spain and Greece, these were not a great danger. The allies did not go to war with each other until the Crimean War in 1854. However, there were still differences and failures. Alexander I's proposal for a Holy Alliance did not work and the Congress System lasted only 10 years. But the failures of the Congress of Vienna were less important than the successes. The self-interest of the members resulted in a long-lasting balance of power.

Examiner's tip This essay meets the criteria of knowledge, argument and relevance. It is well organised. The reasoning can be followed clearly through successive paragraphs. The conclusion rounds it off successfully. A less successful answer would have mentioned a lot of facts without analysing their significance.

Question 2

Examiner's tip The key phrase is 'most important statesman'. This involves an assessment of Metternich's career. 'To what extent' needs a discussion of his achievements and failures and there must be some comparative element.

Although his career was to end in failure, Metternich defended the interests of the Austrian empire with a high degree of success for more than 20 years and he made a major contribution to the maintenance of international peace. In comparison with his contemporaries, he can be regarded as the most important European statesman of his time. Droz was correct in claiming that Metternich stamped his mark on European politics.

The measure of his success can be seen in the length of his period of office. He was in power longer than any contemporary statesman. His early career was shaped by the struggle against Napoleon and, although Britain and Russia might have claimed to have contributed more to the defeat of France, it was Metternich who presided over the meeting of victors at the Congress of Vienna. His influence increased after 1821 when he became Austrian Chancellor and remained largely intact until he was driven from office by the 1848 revolutions. During his long career, he had to deal with many different forces, from the aggression of Napoleon to the disruption of nationalism and liberalism of the 1840s.

Examiner's tip	A good start. The first two paragraphs outline his career relevantly and focus on the argument. The brief reference to Droz shows an intelligent use of reading.

However, his claim to be regarded as the most important statesman of his time was based on more than his long period of office. At the Congress of Vienna (1814–15), he had to deal with other statesmen who had their own ambitions for their countries and whose ideas conflicted. United only in their hatred of Napoleonic France, Tsar Alexander I of Russia, Castlereagh of Britain, Hardenberg of Prussia and Talleyrand of France had different views about post-war Europe. Metternich played off these statesmen against each other, using spies and agents to discover their policies and managing to secure a settlement which very largely met Austria's ambitions. No country was completely satisfied but, most important, every country secured enough to ensure its agreement. Austria conceded the Netherlands as a part of a united kingdom of Holland but its compensating gains in Italy balanced this loss. Lombardy and Venetia helped to establish Austrian power in Italy while Austrian princes were installed in Parma, Modena and Tuscany. Only Piedmont remained largely independent. In Germany, the Confederation of 39 states was placed under the presidency of Austria while the other terms represented a balance of power in which none of Austria's rivals predominated. The dangers of nationalism and liberalism, which might have threatened the complex Austrian empire, were suppressed. Overall, Metternich had most reason to be satisfied with the peace treaty at Vienna.

He continued to see this balance in international affairs as the best safeguard for Austria's interests. When Alexander I proposed the Holy Alliance as a guarantee of peace, Metternich dismissed it as a 'high-sounding nothing' but was willing to go along with the scheme in order to conciliate the tsar because he agreed with the basic principle of ensuring international order. More important was Metternich's support for meetings, or congresses, to settle disputes by agreement. The Congress System failed by 1825 but Metternich had used the meetings to oppose the dangers of unrest in Spain and Italy which might directly threaten international peace and indirectly harm Austria's interests.

Although the German Confederation might be seen as the first step to a united Germany, to which Metternich was opposed, it was used initially as a means of preserving Austrian influence and, as long as he was in office, Metternich used it to curb, not encourage, German nationalism, He imposed the Carlsbad Decrees (1819) which increased censorship and controlled universities with their subversive students. There were further risings in the 1830s and, in 1832, Austria secured the passing of the Six Acts which further increased repression. Metternich persuaded German princes to introduce more restrictive methods of government. Although Prussia was the major German state, its influence was never as strong as Austria's during these years.

In Italy, Metternich was unable to use a central body such as the German Bund to carry out his policies but he intervened constantly to suppress disorder and defeat nationalists. From 1815 to 1848, different Italian groups tried to promote nationalism and there were risings in the 1820s and 1830s but they made little headway. The explanation for this lack of success was partly the divisions between the Italians themselves but much of the credit must go to Metternich for his success in backing the rulers and persuading them to take a tough line against disorder. When Italian states tried to unite against Austria, Metternich divided them by threats and bribes, while the papacy was a firm ally of Catholic Austria.

Examiner's tip The essay has avoided narrative, concentrating instead on the argument. The answer is well organised. Facts are used to support the argument.

Metternich's control was not complete. He could not prevent the outbreak and ultimate success of the Greek revolt against the Ottoman empire while Belgian independence (1830–39) overturned one of the terms of the Vienna settlement. In 1830 a revolution broke out in Poland against Russia but was suppressed harshly and Metternich's vision of a balance in eastern Europe was preserved.

Metternich's downfall came in 1848. His initial reaction to the revolutions in France and Hungary was to use the same methods which had been successful previously. He tried to persuade the Emperor Ferdinand and German princes such as Frederick William IV of Prussia to stand firm but the weak Ferdinand gave in to the increasing unrest and, faced by the probability of dismissal, Metternich fled into exile.

Nevertheless, his final failure does not disguise the fact that he had been for so long the most important figure in European affairs. By comparison, Alexander I was less important and, although ruling such a powerful country, his policies were inconsistent and impractical. France was ruled by a succession of kings who were incapable of playing a major role on the European stage, while Britain's interest was not continuous. None of the German princes enjoyed a comparable influence. Metternich's policies may be seen to have been largely repressive but he thought that these were the best means of defending the interests of Austria and the settlement over which he presided at Vienna was largely successful in maintaining peace in Europe for 40 years and, in some respects, for longer.

Examiner's tip The essay ends by considering alternatives – his failures. The conclusion is an overall summary and compares Metternich with others briefly but effectively. The answer is clearly written; it avoids unnecessary discussion. The essay meets all the criteria of a very good answer.

Question 3

Examiner's tip This requires a comparative approach and covers a wide chronological span. Avoid a narrative approach but explain briefly what happened in 1814–15, 1830 and 1848–9. You should attempt this question only if you know something about all three stages. The discussion should always be related to Vienna.

Examiner's answer plan
The introduction should explain how the Vienna settlement tried to ensure international peace. Indicate which was the more important threat: the 1830 or 1848–9 revolutions. Deal with that first, then deal with the significance of the other. The conclusion should include an overall assessment of the threat of disorder and summarise how far the Vienna settlement survived in 1849. '1830' refers to more than France. There was a revolution in Belgium, risings in Germany

and Poland, and Greece had broken free from the Ottoman empire. '1848–9' should include Austria, Hungary, Germany, France and Italy.

Question 4

Examiner's tip A two-part question. Examiners will expect a reasonable balance. The first part is largely descriptive, requiring an explanation of the aims of the Congress System, where the meetings were held and the issues involved. The second part is more complex and therefore will contribute more to the higher marks.

Examiner's answer plan

• Part 1: Explain why the Congress System was established. Who were its members? In what ways was it a 'System'?

• Part 2: Examine the different aims of the major powers. Explain particularly why Britain opposed intervention in other countries' internal affairs. Link the successive crises to the Congress meetings using analysis and not narrative. How strong is the claim that the System had ended by 1827?

Question 5

Examiner's tip The key phrases are 'European powers suspicious' and 'Russia's intentions'. The question is in two parts: devote about equal time to each. Note the dates.

Examiner's answer plan

An introduction should consider the condition of the Ottoman empire and explain why it created the opportunity for Russian expansion. What were Russia's aims? Analyse the policies to the Eastern Question of other European powers: Austria, Britain, France. Why were they suspicious of Russia? Use the critical events from 1825 to 1856 to show the rivalries between the states. A large part of the answer can deal with the Crimean War, but do not begin in 1854.

Question 6

Examiner's tip A structured essay. The length of each sub-answer should be guided by the mark allocation and by the specific instructions in the question. Do not repeat yourself in different sections.

Examiner's answer plan

Every question asks you to 'explain' something. Part **(a)** should be limited to a brief assessment of Turkey/Ottoman empire; **(b)** requires specific discussion of Russian interests, e.g. a common (Orthodox) religion, access to the Mediterranean; **(c)** should mention individual countries, e.g. Britain felt its Mediterranean interests threatened; **(d)** should be precise about the Straits Convention (1841), closing the Straits to foreign warships; and in **(e)** the key word is 'immediate'. Avoid unnecessary background.

8   NATIONALISM AND UNIFICATION: ITALY AND GERMANY

Question 1

> **Examiner's tip**   The key word is 'architect'. Candidates should know Cavour's career and policies but an unselective narrative will not merit a high mark. The highest marks will be obtained by those who can use the key word as the basis of an analytical answer. 'How far' allows other factors to be considered.

Cavour was indeed the main architect of a united Italy but he did not lay the foundations and the finished building looked very different from what he had planned. There were other architects who often competed with Cavour, and the new Italy reflected both his work and the contributions of others. Although his influence was strong and his design was clear, he had to adapt his plans according to changing events and pressures. This was reflected in the disunity of the country in 1870, which was a contrast to Germany where Bismarck was very much the sole architect.

The groundwork had been laid by others, especially Mazzini, and Cavour could not ignore this when he was appointed Prime Minister in 1852. Nationalism had been growing since 1815 with movements such as the Carbonari. Revolts in the 1820s and in 1831 showed dissatisfaction. However, these risings usually sought only the end of Austrian power in Italy and there was little thought of unification. The regions were very independent, the north being very different from the south. There was no agreement about the design of the future Italy. Some, such as Gioberti, were federalists, favouring a country in which different states would retain many of their powers.

> **Examiner's tip**   The first paragraph is an interesting introduction. It uses the key word 'architect' to suggest ideas. The comparison with Bismarck will be given credit because it is appropriate and brief. You should avoid long-winded comparisons which lead to irrelevance. The second paragraph develops the ideas of the introduction.

Mazzini had a clear plan for Italy. He favoured the unity of all Italy in a republic and he knew how he wished to achieve it. 'Young Italy' was intended to unite Italians against Austria and he felt confident that the strength of the moral case for a unified country was sufficiently convincing to persuade all Italians to rise. However, his plans never came to fruition. The 1848 revolutions, after initial successes, were suppressed by Austria. Radetsky was a capable Austrian general and he defeated the rebel forces at Custozza and Novara. The establishment of the Roman Republic was opposed by Catholic France and Louis Napoleon sent soldiers to restore the city to the Pope.

Garibaldi largely supported Mazzini's plans and his aims were also frustrated. He defended the Roman Republic against France but had to admit defeat. Charles Albert failed in his effort to spread unity from Piedmont while Pius IX contradicted his earlier liberal reputation by opposing revolution.

In 1849, all of the plans of the previous architects of Italian unity seem to have failed. Nevertheless, they had done much to awaken Italy to the call for freedom from Austria and the people were more ready to consider the plans of Cavour.

The term 'architect' suggests that Cavour deliberately intended to bring about the unity of Italy but this would be an exaggeration. His original plan was to expand the influence of Piedmont in the north of Italy. He was conservative rather than radical in opinion and distrusted those who had failed in 1848. In strengthening Piedmont, he was able to use its economic strength as the most progressive state in Italy. Railways were improved. Trade treaties with other European countries made them more aware of the importance of Piedmont. Victor Emmanuel II was determined to succeed where Charles Albert had failed. A monarch would reassure other European rulers who distrusted a republican Italy while his limited powers, because he ruled under a constitution, made him more acceptable to other Italians who might not have been willing to be ruled by a despotic king.

Cavour knew how he intended to carry out his blue-print of expansion but his methods were different from those which had failed Mazzini. He realised that Austria could only be defeated with the help of more powerful states. Italy could not unify itself and the slogan 'Farà da sè' was rejected. His first step was to involve Piedmont in the Crimean War (1854–6). Although Piedmont's contribution was small and nothing was gained in the Treaty of Paris, Cavour had succeeded in winning recognition from more powerful European countries. Napoleon III was sympathetic to Italian nationalism and had previously supported the Carbonari. Piedmont's participation in the Crimean War and an attempted assassination persuaded Napoleon to agree to give help at Plombières (1858). Cavour was sensible enough to realise that he had to concede something to enable him to complete his plans. Nice and Savoy were given to France and, although Napoleon betrayed him at Villafranca, Cavour was able soon afterwards to gain the states of Parma, Modena, Tuscany and the Romagna. He was careful to make it seem as if he was not imposing his plans on these states but manipulated plebiscites to demonstrate popular support for the link with Piedmont.

At this point, it seemed as if Cavour's plans had been successful because Italy in 1860 resembled closely his design. However, other forces made him change his plans. The republican Garibaldi invaded the south and marched on Rome after conquering Sicily and Naples, which Victor Emmanuel II and Cavour saw as dangerous. Garibaldi was a rival rather than an ally and he regarded the cession of Nice and Savoy to France as a betrayal of Italy. Rome was important to Catholics and its seizure would harm the interests of Piedmont which wished to be a respected power in Europe. Reluctantly, Cavour decided to change his plans and he persuaded Garibaldi to give up his gains so that Italy now included the south as well as the north. Only Rome and Venetia remained outside.

Italy was unfinished when Cavour died in 1861 and it was not completed until 1870. He had done most to design Italy. Italy was a monarchy and the republican hopes of Mazzini and Garibaldi were frustrated. Piedmont was the strongest state but it did not dominate Italy as Prussia dominated the newly unified Germany. He was indeed the main architect although he did not have full control over the end product.

Examiner's tip The discussion of Cavour is effective. It pursues a line of argument and the candidate comments on developments. The essay will get credit for pointing out how much Cavour had achieved by his death and what was done afterwards. Relevant and well-organised, it considers alternatives.

Question 2

Examiner's tip Select your knowledge to answer the questions precisely. Avoid unnecessary introductions or conclusions. The questions are based on the Austro-Prussian rivalry. Use other knowledge only when it is very relevant to this.

(a) Four German states were Bavaria, Hanover, Prussia and Saxony. [1 mark each.]

(b) The Schleswig-Holstein Question secured the cooperation of Austria which would not allow Prussia to act alone against Denmark. [Good opening statement – 1 mark.] Bismarck used an old grievance about the treatment of Austrians and Germans in Schleswig-Holstein to foment a quarrel with Denmark but an alliance with Austria would reassure that country that Bismarck was not a danger to the balance of power in Germany. The swift victory had other, more indirect, significance because it strengthened Bismarck's hold over Prussia, which was to be important when next he moved against Austria. [2 marks for immediate significance.] The liberals in the parliament had opposed the budget with its greater spending on the military. Prussia became united and Bismarck could use this as a basis for future action. The issue persuaded Bismarck that other countries, which had not opposed the actions of Austria and Prussia to defend an agreement about Danish control of Schleswig-Holstein, might not intervene in the future if he took further steps against Austria. [2 marks for longer term effects.]

(c) By 1867, Austria was defeated by Prussia in the Seven Weeks' War (1866) and was excluded from Germany in the Peace of Prague which established the North German Confederation. [1 mark for precise reference.] The treaty confirmed Prussia as the major state in Germany although the largely Catholic states of the south were still outside its direct control and several of them looked to Austria for protection against Prussian influence. Austria was also lacking in friends elsewhere in Europe. [2 marks.] Bismarck could take advantage of Austria's reputation as the enemy of Italian nationalism and secured Venetia for Italy in the Prague treaty. [1 mark.] Russia and Austria were traditional rivals in the Balkans and Alexander II became more sympathetic to Prussia when Bismarck cooperated over the Polish revolt of 1863. Britain was reluctant to intervene. Most important, Bismarck secured the neutrality of France at Biarritz. His deception of Napoleon III prevented Austria gaining the potentially important alliance of France. [3 marks for development.]

(d) Bismarck was careful in the Treaty of Prague not to punish Austria unduly. He secured his immediate aim of excluding Austria from influence in Germany and imposed comparatively minor territorial concessions. Austria lost Holstein and Venetia. [2 marks for immediate situation.] However, Bismarck was careful not to alienate his enemy and used two means of ending Austro-Prussian rivalry. Having lost its influence in Germany, Austria was encouraged to develop its interests in the Balkans and Bismarck included Austria in his system of alliances which was designed to neutralise France after 1870. [2 marks for Bismarck's policy.] Austria and Germany joined with Russia in the League of the Three Emperors (Dreikaiserbund, 1873) and in 1879 they agreed the Dual Alliance. During the changing diplomacy of Bismarck's later career, his wish to retain the friendship of Austria remained constant and this was largely successful in erasing the memory of the earlier rivalry. [2 marks for development.] For its part, Austria felt that it had little alternative to closer relations with Germany. Relations with Russia were never close in spite of the Dreikaiserbund and, while friendship with France was a possibility, Bismarck was successful in keeping the two apart. This alliance survived the fall of Bismarck and the decision of Kaiser William II to direct policy himself, forming a cornerstone of the Triple Alliance. [3 marks for showing outcome.]

Question 3

Examiner's tip   'Why?' asks for reasons. Although Cavour is important, an answer which explains only his career will have limited value. Continue the discussion after his death (1861).

Examiner's answer plan

The introduction should explain the strengths of Piedmont: independence from Austria, situated in richest part of Italy, Charles Albert a sympathetic monarch. Analyse the condition of Italy and explain why alternatives failed, e.g. Mazzini, Gioberti. What were the lessons of 1848 for Piedmont? Role of Victor Emmanuel II. Develop to explain how Cavour unified the northern states under Piedmont. Emphasise his methods to explain events. The conclusion should show how the rest of Italy was united from 1861 to 1870.

Question 4

> **Examiner's tip**   The quotation must be the focus of the answer. You do not have to agree but you must consider its implications before discussing alternatives. Note the key dates: 1861–70.

Examiner's answer plan

Explain briefly the condition of Italy in 1861; avoid unnecessary background about events unless related to specified period, that is to explain divisions of 1861–70. Examine the social/political/religious divisions: rich and poor regions; differences between monarchists and republicans; papalists and those who wanted to incorporate Rome. Develop by examining how far 1861–70 saw 'accidental' developments, e.g. impact of the wars between Prussia and Austria/Prussia and France. Conclude by assessing 'vocal minority'. What were the different aims of groups?

Question 5

> **Examiner's tip**   The key issue is the assessment of Garibaldi. Mazzini, Cavour, etc will only be relevant if linked to Garibaldi. A very good answer will go further than a description of his military exploits; it will assess their effects. The key phrase is 'only contribution'.

Examiner's answer plan

Outline Garibaldi's aims, always linking developments and events to the issues of unification, e.g. support for Mazzini. Explain 'his skill as a soldier' using particularly the Roman Republic and the Naples–Sicily expedition. Assess the contribution of Garibaldi's exploits to Italian unification, e.g. failure in 1848–9 and success in 1860. Assess alternative explanations: his reputation in Europe, gaining support from other European countries, personal charisma.

Question 6

> **Examiner's tip**   A structured essay. The length of each sub-answer should be guided by the mark allocation and by the specific instructions in the question. Note the different instructions: 'What ... Explain ... To what extent ... Did ...'.

Examiner's answer plan

(a) The key word is Germany. Avoid a general description of Vienna.

(b) The emphasis is on causes, not results ('establishment of the German Confederation').

(c) Concentrate on the gains for Prussia; territorial and influence over smaller states. Then compare with gains for other states, e.g. Austria and presidency of Confederation.

(d) Key phrase is 'lay the foundations'. Later developments will not be relevant. After explaining Vienna, consider other factors, e.g. Zollverein.

Question 7

> **Examiner's tip** The question suggests two possible explanations. An answer which assumes that one is correct and ignores the other will get lower marks. Before writing, decide which is more justified and discuss this first, then the other.

Examiner's answer plan

- Introduction should justify which claim is more valid.
- 'Reacted to events' should include provocation by Prussian liberals over budget; Napoleon III's eagerness for gains on the Rhineland led to French neutrality in war against Austria; Spanish dispute opened way to Franco-Prussian War.
- 'Long-term plans' should include development of Bismarck's policies and relationship with Austria – Schleswig-Holstein dispute; war followed by North German Confederation; war followed by full unity.
- Conclusion should indicate how far each claim is true, assessing relative weights.

Question 8

> **Examiner's tip** Balance the answer evenly between Bismarck and Cavour and concentrate on relations with Austria. Note that this is a comparison question. Do not write two sequential accounts with a brief comparative conclusion.

Examiner's answer plan

Introduction should explain why Austria posed a problem to Bismarck/Prussia and Cavour/Piedmont. Discuss Bismarck's alliance with Austria against Denmark, then war, then moderate peace. Cavour could not ally with Austria; was forced to seek alliance with France. Bismarck isolated Austria and secured neutrality from other states. Cavour could not isolate Austria himself but obtained support. Bismarck could use Prussian army. Piedmont's army was weak and Cavour had to use French army and other methods.

9 FRANCE, 1815–70

Question 1

> **Examiner's tip** The key words are 'most successful'. You should not write a narrative description of events from 1815 to 1870 but concentrate on an assessment of the rulers. Explain first the most successful, justifying your priority. Then deal with others in order of success.

It is easy to decide who was the least successful ruler of France. Charles X ruled for only six years (1824–30) and his reign was marked by complete failure. However, it is necessary to make clear the criteria for success. They had different aims and faced different problems; none of the other rulers was completely successful but they all had their different claims to fame. Napoleon III (1848–70) was both very successful and very unsuccessful. Louis Philippe (1830–48) was not as successful as his successor but he avoided the heavy defeat suffered by Napoleon III. On balance, the most successful was Louis XVIII (1814–24). While he did not achieve as much as his successors, he did not suffer their setbacks.

Examiner's tip This is a sound introduction. It focuses on the main issue: comparative success. The definition of success is exact and the candidate avoids vagueness.

Louis XVIII's biggest claim to be regarded as the most successful ruler of France during this period was that he died as king. The other reigns ended in revolution and abdications but Louis XVIII handed power to his heir and brother, Charles X. His reign was unspectacular but he did much to reconcile his subjects. France was accepted by other countries which had fought against Napoleon.

He was sensible, issuing a Charter which guaranteed rights to his subjects. Whatever he wished privately, he did not show signs of wanting to return to the *ancien regime*, which would have enraged the revolutionaries in France. He believed in divine right but did not use the claim to establish an absolute monarchy. Louis was lucky because the economy improved after the end of the Napoleonic Wars and he benefited from this although his policies were not strictly responsible for the improvement. Ill-health and old age allowed Charles to become more powerful but overall Louis XVIII could have boasted that he achieved most of his aims.

Napoleon III's reign ended in disaster. The defeat by Prussia at Sedan caused his abdication and the end of the empire. He was largely responsible for this because he had been outwitted by Bismarck. He was ambitious and wanted to be admired in France and Europe but he lacked the ability to be a successful statesman.

His greatest claim to success was his domestic policy. Louis Napoleon's popularity enabled him to become President of the Second Republic after the 1848 revolution. His next success was in overthrowing the Republic and establishing himself as emperor in 1851. He gained power by force in a coup d'état but this was accepted by the French. As emperor he had complete authority, choosing ministers and members of the Senate and dictating policy. However, Napoleon III did not rule harshly. The franchise was wide and he was careful to give the impression through plebiscites that he listened to his subjects. Frenchmen found that their standard of living was improving. There were social and economic reforms. More houses were built for the poor while insurance schemes also helped the lower classes. The railway system expanded. Banks were founded. Napoleon III copied the British Great Exhibition of 1851, organising similar exhibitions in France to show its great achievements. Baron Haussmann rebuilt Paris, creating wide avenues.

After 1860, Napoleon III introduced the 'Liberal Empire'. Some historians believe that this was a genuine move to reforms but it is more likely that he revised his rule to weaken the opposition. Concessions were made to politicians and censorship was relaxed. However, although the changes did not affect his ultimate authority as emperor, they did not succeed in deflecting the opposition, which increased in Paris and elsewhere. Thiers ('Five Fundamental Freedoms') and the novelist Victor Hugo were leading critics of the regime. Nevertheless, Napoleon III retained his popularity and he achieved another large vote of confidence in a plebiscite in 1870.

Foreign policy was his downfall. After his early success in the Crimean War he met several failures. He became unpopular in Italy and with French liberals when he withdrew his support for Piedmont after the battle of Solferino. The Mexican campaign was a disaster and alienated all of the other European powers. His most serious failure was in dealing with Bismarck, who was a far more capable statesmen. Napoleon III was defeated diplomatically in the Austro-Prussian War and militarily in the Franco-Prussian War. He quickly fell from power after the battle of Sedan but he had reigned more than 20 years, a longer period than any other ruler from 1815 to 1870.

Examiner's tip The answer has developed into a very interesting argument. The factual references are appropriate and support the argument. The essay continues to concentrate on an assessment of success. The paragraphs on Louis XVIII and Napoleon III are well balanced.

Louis Philippe's claims to success are modest. Although he enjoyed much support in 1830, he wasted his opportunities and failed to unite the different political and social groups in France. He had accepted a limited monarchy but he was aloof from advice. Louis Philippe's policies of free trade and non-intervention which benefited the middle classes did not protect the lower classes from the effects of industrialisation. His ministers, especially Guizot, were unpopular.

People believed that his foreign policy did not protect French interests and his willingness to give in to British pressure over Belgium and the Spanish marriages was a contrast to the glories of Napoleon. He was unfortunate to some extent because economic conditions worsened but he contributed much to his downfall in 1848. His only success was that he had gained power in 1830 and his rule marked the end of divine right.

In a sense, none of the French rulers from 1815 to 1870 was very successful. French politics during this period were very unstable. There were too many different political groups with a tendency to use riots and revolution to achieve their aims and the rulers usually failed to address the most fundamental problems. But the ruler who managed most successfully to avoid trouble and bring stability was Louis XVIII.

Examiner's tip The brief conclusion rounds off the essay satisfactorily. It does not merely repeat what has been written earlier but makes some general points, all related to the question. There are signs of individual judgement here and the candidate has justified the order of priority by explaining the criteria. Factually it is very accurate and the facts are always used effectively to support the argument.

Question 2

Examiner's tip Concentrate on the quotation. It suggests extreme judgements: success–failure. You may agree largely with the claims but examine how far they are justified. A very good answer will examine the limitations as well as the extent of an argument.

Ultimately, Napoleon III must be judged a failure. He was swept from office in the aftermath of the disastrous defeat at Sedan in 1870. As emperor, he had enjoyed full power in France and therefore could not escape blame for disgrace which France had suffered. Furthermore, since the regime was identified so closely with him personally, the empire fell to be replaced by a republican government which represented everything to which he was opposed. Nevertheless, the fall of Napoleon III was sudden and, to some extent, unforeseen. Although there was opposition to his rule in France, he had just won a resounding victory in a plebiscite and it seemed as if the Second Empire might last indefinitely.

Examiner's tip The introduction is a good summary of the reign, highlighting developments. It avoids unnecessary background but suggests interesting lines which will be developed during the essay.

Napoleon III enjoyed significant successes in his domestic policies. He won a very large majority in the election for President of the Second Republic and governed securely from 1848 to 1852. He enjoyed a reputation as a liberal and social reformer which was based on his support for Italian nationalism and his writing about pauperism; he benefited from the Napoleonic Legend, which looked to a leader like Napoleon I who could unify France and make the country powerful in Europe again. His coup d'état of 1851 and the declaration of the empire in 1852 gave him considerable powers which he used with some skill. Although authoritarian, he was not a ruthless dictator. Soon political prisoners were released and he used carefully arranged plebiscites to give the appearance of democracy. There was a Senate but it was controlled by the emperor while the parliament had few powers. Local officials came under his control but the system was justified because it resembled that of Napoleon I.

Napoleon III provided greater economic prosperity and improved social conditions. Public works, such as the building of roads, created employment while the railways expanded, encouraging trade. New banks were founded and people invested in industry. The emperor encouraged large public buildings and much of Paris was rebuilt by Haussmann. Although it is not clear how far these improvements were directly the work of Napoleon III, his government helped to create the conditions that made them possible.

After 1860, the 'Liberal Empire' introduced reforms which eased the system of press censorship and made ministers more answerable to public opinion. Parliament was given more control over finances and the franchise was extended. These measures may have been forced on Napoleon III by growing opposition but they did not represent a significant weakening of his position. Even the constitutional changes which were suggested in 1870 would only have limited his powers slightly. Considering the balance of his successes and failures at home, one must conclude that the former far outweighed the latter.

Examiner's tip The section on domestic policy discusses the quotation relevantly. Although it sees Napoleon III as largely successful, it also considers some of his failures.

However, whatever achievements he enjoyed domestically were outweighed by his disasters abroad. As Grenville has claimed, Napoleon III wished 'to make France as far as possible the centre of European diplomacy'. Unfortunately, he lacked the ability to do so. His aims were never consistent and he misjudged those with whom he had to deal, especially Bismarck. The 1860s saw a series of setbacks until the last, and most serious, defeat of 1870.

His first foreign engagement seemed to promise that he could indeed make France the leading diplomatic power in Europe. The Crimean War ended with a peace conference at Paris in 1856 and, although France gained no territory and Napoleon III was not particularly successful as a peace-maker, the meeting gave the impression that France had restored peace, increasing his prestige in Europe and his popularity in France. From this point, setback followed setback. He had long been attracted to the cause of Italian unification and agreed to back Cavour against Austria. He saw a united Italy as a grateful friend of France which would extend French influence in the Mediterranean. The failure of an assassination plot convinced the emperor that he was destined to be the saviour of Italy – and there was also the hope of territorial advantage. At Plombières in 1858, he gained from Cavour the promise of Nice and Savoy but the battles of Magenta and Solferino changed his mind. To avoid being caught up in a long and wasteful war, he deserted Cavour and made a separate peace with Austria at Villafranca in 1859. Although he later gained Nice and Savoy, the episode had only served to lose him the trust of French liberals and the friendship of Italy. Italians were further alienated when French troops protected the Pope in Rome until 1870.

Napoleon III's attempt to put the Austrian prince, Maximilian, on the throne of a French empire in Mexico resulted in a fiasco (1863–7). The French army was defeated by the Mexicans and Maximilian was shot, which horrified Austria, while Britain became suspicious of French expanionism. The episode revealed to other European powers such as Prussia and Russia how limited were Napoleon's abilities as an international statesman. When there was a rebellion of Poland, it was Bismarck not Napoleon III who offered help to the Russian tsar.

Most crucially, Napoleon was first outwitted and then defeated by Bismarck. He was convinced that the impending war between Austria and Prussia would be a long struggle and that France could be the arbitrator, benefiting from its mediation. He had hopes for gains in the Rhineland. In 1865 at Biarritz, Bismarck did nothing to shake this opinion but persuaded the emperor to be neutral. The Prussian victory left Napoleon III without any gains and his secret ambitions, which Bismarck published, caused anger among the German states. By 1870, Napoleon III was without allies in Europe while Bismarck had no enemies except France. The other countries were either friendly to Prussia or neutral. It was not difficult for Bismarck to stir up French public opinion when it seemed as if Napoleon III had been insulted over the affair of the Spanish marriages. The Empress Eugenie, the French press and almost all French public opinion pressed for war and Bismarck managed easily to make it appear as if France, not Prussia, was the aggressor. The Franco-Prussian War proved the superiority of the modern Prussian army over the French, but Napoleon III had already been outwitted before the war began.

Overall, there can be no doubt that Napoleon III was internationally a failure. Unfortunately for him and the empire over which he ruled, his considerable domestic successes did not matter when his country had been conquered by Prussia.

Examiner's tip A very good answer. It is thoroughly relevant, well organised and analytical in approach. The argument develops logically. Accurate knowledge is selected to underpin the points which are made.

Question 3

Examiner's tip 'Explain' requires you to discuss the reasons for the 1830 revolution. You can include developments from 1815, but the reign of Louis XVIII will be relevant only if related to the question.

Examiner's answer plan

An introduction should show the events of 1830, concentrating on why these brought about the revolution and abdication of Charles X. Explain Charles X's aims. How did he try to reintroduce absolute monarchy? His use of ministers and measures before 1830 will show why he became increasingly unpopular. Examine the different political groupings in France, e.g. republicans, Bonapartists, moderate royalists. A good answer will also assess the importance of economic changes; there was widespread distress.

Question 4

Examiner's tip A structured essay. The length of each sub-answer should be guided by the mark allocation and by the specific instructions in the question. Be exact in your answers. Do not repeat yourself in different sections.

Examiner's answer plan

(a) Be exact and do not waste time by providing more than one policy of Charles X.

(b) Ultras were the extreme royalists who wanted to restore much of pre-1789 France.

(c) Only 3 marks available so concentrate on situation in 1830 and just previously.

(d) Louis Philippe was a compromise candidate – explain why. He avoided extreme views and had sympathies with changes since 1789. France did not favour a republic.

(e) The key phrase is 'King of the French', i.e. reflected end of divine right, his election as king, limited power. These points should be developed in one paragraph.

Question 5

Examiner's tip 'How accurate' means that you must test the truth of the quotation. Decide how far you agree with it and make your argument clear at the beginning. Present the points in favour and those against in order of your priority.

Examiner's answer plan

Showman – Napoleon III enjoyed display at home and wanted to play an important role as an influential foreign statesman. Dictator – explain and assess how far he enjoyed power at home. How significant were the changes after 1860? The phrase as a whole denotes that his rule was shallow and his abilities limited. The essay allows for a discussion of domestic and foreign policies but it should analyse developments in the light of the description in the question.

Question 6

Examiner's tip 'Why?' asks for reasons. These include the errors of Napoleon III but a good answer will also deal with Bismarck. Focus on the situation in 1870 and relate earlier developments to this.

Examiner's answer plan
The introduction should indicate Napoleon III's isolation in 1870: lacked support from Austria, Britain, Russia, Italy. The essay can develop to show how and why he alienated these countries. How far was this isolation due to the policies of Bismarck, who was careful not to offend other countries? This analytical approach will deserve a higher mark than an answer which contains a chronological survey from 1852.

10 CAUSES OF THE FIRST WORLD WAR, 1871–1914

Question 1

Examiner's tip The question involves an assessment of the quotation. How far is it justified? The answer should begin by explaining the role of Germany before examining other issues. This approach will gain a higher mark than a general account of the causes of the First World War.

When Germany and its allies were defeated in the First World War, the victorious countries were sure which country should be blamed for its outbreak. The War Guilt clause in the Treaty of Versailles and the penalties imposed on Germany seemed justified because it was most responsible for a war which had killed millions of people. Different views were later expressed as historians considered the roles of other countries, but the Fischer thesis revived the claim about German guilt.

However, it may seem unlikely that one country alone was responsible for causing a war which involved every important country in the world. The Balkans Crisis of 1914 was not of Germany's making and other states contributed to international tensions by increasing their arms. Nevertheless, in weighing the comparative responsibilities of different states, it appears that Germany, more than any other country, caused the First World War.

Examiner's tip The first two paragraphs are very promising. They focus immediately on Germany, they refer briefly to alternative explanations and they make clear the candidate's fundamental argument.

Kaiser William II took over control of German foreign policy in 1890 and immediately began to adopt more aggressive policies. Resenting Britain's naval supremacy, he embarked on a rapid increase of the German navy that alarmed Britain, which William II should have realised because Britain's power rested on its navy. It was also unnecessary because Britain had no interests on the continent. However, William II wanted Germany to become a world power, expanding its colonies and influence abroad. His tactlessness, for example in congratulating Kruger on the failure of the Jameson Raid, made it seem that he did not mind offending Britain. When he visited Morocco and then sent a warship to Agadir (1911), he was threatening both Britain and France. As a result, he made an enemy of Britain and encouraged its cooperation with France.

The Kaiser strengthened the alliance with Austria-Hungary and therefore lost the friendship of Russia, Austria-Hungary's rival in the Balkans. Germany itself had no direct interests in the Balkans but it supported Austria-Hungary in its quarrels with the Serbs and, after the assassination of Franz Ferdinand at Sarajevo, gave its ally a 'blank cheque', effectively promising any support that was needed. This meant that Germany lost control in the middle of a crisis because it did not restrain its ally and was dragged into a war. This is not to say that Germany was innocent because it did too little to prevent war and its generals were eager for action. The Schlieffen Plan involved a swift attack on France through Belgium before a quick war. Therefore Germany preferred to fight rather than work out a diplomatic settlement.

William II and his ministers were also guilty of miscalculation because they did not believe that the Balkans Crisis would spread to the rest of Europe and the invasion of Belgium was carried out without a realisation of the consequences for Britain. For many years, but especially after the 'War Council' of 1912, William II and his advisers had carried out risky policies. Europe had been on the edge of war several times, for example in 1906 and 1911, and Germany was largely responsible for these crises.

| **Examiner's tip** | The section on Germany is organised and persuasive. It argues a clear case. The facts are used to support a good argument and it shows the development of German policy. |

Austria-Hungary must also bear much of the blame. Although it was acting defensively in trying to prevent the break-up of its empire in the face of relentless nationalist attacks, it over-reacted in 1914. The murder of Franz Ferdinand, the heir to the throne, was obviously a major blow and Austria-Hungary saw the Serbs as terrorists who would only be halted by military action. In the eyes of Austria-Hungary, they had broken a series of treaties and their word could not be trusted. Nevertheless, the demands made on Serbia after the assassination were so harsh that Austria-Hungary probably intended them not to be accepted. They were just an excuse for war. When Germany gave its support, Austria-Hungary could not be restrained from trying to teach Serbia a harsh lesson.

The responsibility of the members of the Triple Entente was more indirect. Russia resented Austria-Hungary's attempts to bully the Serbs and was determined to protect the minor nationalities. It also wanted to regain the prestige which had been lost in the war against Japan (1904–5). The country had a large army and the generals felt sure that they could defeat Austria-Hungary. They probably did not think that they would face the German army as well. Although we know that the Russian army was inefficient, this was not fully realised at the time and Russian mobilisation showed the determination of Nicholas II, his ministers and generals not to back down.

France and Britain bear even less direct responsibility. France had contributed to the deterioration in international relations by its thirst for revenge against Germany after the defeat of Sedan (1870). It was determined to regain Alsace Lorraine. But Bismarck had largely succeeded in keeping France isolated and it was the policies of William II which had allowed France to ally with Russia and Britain. When Russia entered the war, France saw the opportunity to win back what had been lost. Britain had few direct interests in the Balkans or even in the rest of the continent. However, it was determined to defend Belgian independence and the German invasion of Belgium caused Britain to declare war. Possibly Britain could have made clearer to Germany what would happen if Germany attacked Belgium but it is equally likely that the German government would not have listened. The Kaiser had backed down over North Africa and was under pressure not to do so again.

Overall, it is true that we need look no further than Berlin. Although Germany was not the only guilty country, its responsibility far outweighed that of other countries. The Kaiser's ambitions were too extreme. Without Germany, it is likely that 1914 would have been just another Balkan Crisis.

The above answer contains a variety of points. It is well organised and well structured. It will gain credit for discussing alternatives. The roles of different countries are assessed critically.

Question 2

The key phrases are 'system of alliances and ententes' and 'outbreak of war'. Your essay can discuss other causes but must first assess the suggested explanation. The focus should be on 1914 and background material will only be given credit when related to this.

The assassination of Franz Ferdinand at Sarajevo in June 1914 set in motion a series of events which ended with the outbreak of a general European war by the middle of August. The antagonists were members of two groups which had been rivals since the beginning of the twentieth century. In the Triple Alliance, Germany fought on the side of Austria-Hungary against the Triple Entent's Britain, France and Russia. Nevertheless, although the system of alliances and ententes had contributed to the growing tensions of the preceding period, its influence was limited during the critical period leading to the beginning of the war.

Germany and Austria-Hungary were firm allies, the former being the leader, and it was Germany's 'blank cheque' which encouraged Austria-Hungary to push to the limit its demands against Serbia. However, Italy had never been a committed member of the Triple Alliance; Austria was Italy's traditional enemy because of its role in suppressing nationalism in the nineteenth century. In spite of being a member of the Triple Alliance, Italy made agreements with France and Russia in the early twentieth century, promising not to fight unless attacked, and it did not join its partners in going to war in 1914. In the following year, Italy deserted the Triple Alliance and joined its enemies in the Triple Entente. Therefore, the relationship between Germany and Austria-Hungary reflected more the Dual Alliance of 1879, created by Bismarck, than the Triple Alliance.

The effectiveness of the Triple Entente in the summer of 1914 was also limited. Russia took the initiative, mobilising in defence of Serbia, but France was directly involved only when it was attacked by Germany as part of the Schlieffen Plan. Its response to German demands for neutrality were imprecise and it did not immediately come to the aid of its Entente partner. Germany did not assume that the Entente countries would act together but its military strategy was based on first knocking out France before fighting a war against Russia. Britain entered the war not because of the Balkans dispute or because Russia was a fellow member of the Triple Entente but because the Schlieffen Plan involved an attack on France through Belgium whose independence Britain was pledged to defend. Therefore, in a real sense, the Franco-Russian Dual Alliance of the late nineteenth century was more important in 1914 than the Triple Alliance.

These paragraphs have introduced the alliances and contain a good argument, assessing their importance in a critical manner. The essay is taking a strong and interesting line. A promising start.

During these criticial weeks, the determination of Austria-Hungary to crush Serbian independence, supported by a militarist Germany, was most responsible for the outbreak of war. It could have been envisaged that Russia would support Serbia although Germany hoped that it would back down again as it had done during the Balkan Wars of 1912–13. In turn, Russia mobilised and diplomacy failed to defuse the situation as had happened previously.

The Triple Alliance and Triple Entente were not highly organised coalitions. Military strategies were not coordinated and each member had its different aims and priorities. Germany, under William II, was determined to become a world power. The enmity with France, dating from 1870, continued as a consistent factor in international diplomacy but the hostility between Germany and Britain developed when Germany embarked on a naval race, threatening British domination at sea. The Kaiser's intervention in South and North Africa strained relations further. The Kaiser was unpredictable and came increasingly under the influence of aggressive generals and politicians. Overall, Germany did not shape its policies to suit Austria-Hungary.

Austria-Hungary justified its policies as defensive actions against the disruptive Balkan states, seeing Russia as provoking the nationalities such as the Serbs. Although relying on German support, it pursued independent policies. Italy was pre-occupied with the attempt to gain Tangier from France; its interest was purely national and it was a member of the Triple Alliance in little more than name only.

In the Triple Entente, French foreign policy was based on an anti-German stance following defeat in 1870 and the loss of Alsace-Lorraine. Relations deteriorated further when the Kaiser appeared to threaten French interests in North Africa, for example in the Moroccan Crises of 1906 and 1911. There were some positive reasons for France's friendship with Russia, for example there were large French investments in the Russian economy, but their alliance was one of convenience rather than of close interest. France was an enemy of Germany rather than of Austria-Hungary while Russia was a rival more of Austria-Hungary than of Germany. Indeed Bismarck had managed to retain the friendship of both countries and it was William II who chose Austria-Hungary as an ally rather than Russia choosing Germany as an enemy.

Britain was not anxious to get closely involved in the affairs of the continent. There was a possibility of an Anglo-German agreement in the late nineteenth century until William II embarked on his competitive policies. Britain and France patched up their former differences and came closer in the Entente Cordiale of 1904, followed by a similar British agreement with Russia. However, these alliances were not an important element of British foreign policy to 1914 and there were no formal undertakings to go to war on behalf of an entente partner.

Examiner's tip The development of the essay shows how each country viewed the alliances. The approach is analytical. Background material, e.g. 1906, 1911, is used relevantly and does not merely narrate events.

Nevertheless, the existence of the two alliances reflected the uneasy peace in Europe in the early twentieth century. Crises in North Africa and the Balkans were dangerous because they threatened to become wars which would involve more than two countries. It could not be assumed that a conflict involving, for example, Austria-Hungary and Russia, would not drag in the other powers. The large-scale increase in armaments, the use of railway for military purposes and the plans for mobilisation made it less likely that hostilities could be localised.

Although the system of alliances and ententes was not directly responsible for the outbreak of war in 1914 – this was more the responsibility of individual states – it had done much to shape the international situation and to prepare the way for war. Instead of safeguarding peace and promoting defence, their original purpose, the alliances gave countries the confidence that would enable them to go to war.

Examiner's tip A very good mark will be awarded because the answer is thoroughly relevant and analytical. It considers different ideas. The emphasis is on assessment rather than description and the answer always focuses on 1914.

Question 3

Examiner's tip 'To what extent' allows for other interpretations of German foreign policy but you must first discuss the key words 'dangerously' *and* 'aggressive'. A reasonable proportion of the answer must be on the period before 1914.

Examiner's answer plan
Introduce the aims of William II. Explain how his character influenced his policies. 'Aggressive' might include policy at sea, North Africa, Middle East, willingness to support Austria-Hungary in the Balkans. A very good answer will deal with military strategy and the role of ministers, military leaders. Examine the crises, explaining why they were dangerous. Discussion of 1914 should assess Germany's responsibility.

Question 4

Examiner's tip Largely a two-part question and your answer should be divided equally between Morocco and the Balkans. The focus must be on the role in 'the outbreak of war'.

Examiner's answer plan
Morocco showed German willingness to be more active in international affairs; threatened British and French interests and confirmed their entente. Germany was determined not to back down again. This had an indirect effect in 1914. Balkans brought in Austria-Hungary and Russia. Showed the instability of the region and how major powers could be involved. Germany was more successful and wished to repeat this success, with Austria-Hungary, in 1914. The conclusion should explain 1914 developments but should link them with previous crises.

Question 5

Examiner's tip The focus should be on the link between the Balkans and 1914. You will need an understanding of Balkans' issues and detailed knowledge of events and of the outbreak of the war. But use the facts to support an argument.

Examiner's answer plan
The introduction should explain the situation in the Balkans. Develop by showing why the major powers were involved. Assess the seriousness of previous crises. The main part of the answer should analyse the factors involved in 1914, beginning with the Balkans. Then show why other

issues became important, e.g. German attack on France, Britain's wish to defend Belgian neutrality. A good conclusion would be an explanation of reasons why the 1914 crisis was not defused as previous disputes had been.

Question 6

Examiner's tip The key word is 'diplomacy'. Although much of the material is similar to that in question 5, it must be organised differently. A very good answer will concentrate on 1914; earlier references will only be given credit if linked to this year.

Examiner's answer plan

An introduction can outline developments in 1914 with the emphasis on why they led to war. Develop the answer by analysing the policies of different countries. How far was each interested in a diplomatic solution? E.g. Austria-Hungary was determined to crush Serbia; Britain favoured diplomacy, but did it make its intentions clear? Show what diplomatic steps were taken. Conclude by explaining the forces against diplomacy, e.g. mobilisation, influence of militarists.

11 RUSSIA AND COMMUNISM, 1905–39

Question 1

Examiner's tip The key phrases are the quotations. These must be used directly in the account of the fall of tsarism. A weak answer will write a general survey of Russia with a brief reference to the quotations, but a good answer will keep the quotations in mind throughout the argument.

The First World War changed Russian history decisively and effectively killed the tsarist regime in Russia. Although the government may have been ill in 1914, even seriously unwell, it was not terminally ill. The effects of the war on Russia may have been particularly disastrous but they were not limited to that country. War also killed the governments of William II of Germany and Francis Joseph of Austria-Hungary and, although the effects on democratic Britain and France were not so extreme, these countries were also changed forever. The First World War unleashed forces far greater and more dangerous than previous conflicts.

Examiner's tip A good introduction. It immediately clarifies which of the quotations it agrees with. It makes some general points about Europe but links them to Russia. Therefore they become directly relevant. This will deserve more credit than an answer which refers to other developments without linking them to the topic.

In 1914 there were warning signs in Russia. The tsar, Nicholas II, was not an efficient ruler and he obstinately opposed all change, believing that the way to deal with opposition was to crush and not appease it by concessions. His court was filled by incompetents who were also reactionary and the tsarina encouraged him not to liberalise Russia. The economy was backward. There was only a small middle class while the peasants were impoverished on their small pieces of land. From 1912, a wave of strikes expressed the dissatisfaction of the working classes.

Nevertheless there were signs of hope. There was still considerable veneration for the tsar. Republicanism was limited to a few extremists whose leaders had usually been arrested or exiled. Nicholas II survived the threat of the 1905 revolution and there was little imminent danger of a revolution in 1914. Although reluctant, he authorised a Duma. The first two meetings were failures because Nicholas largely ignored them but the Third Duma (1912) was more successful. There was cautious optimism in the political situation although Nicholas II would need a lot of persuading to introduce further reforms.

Witte introduced some improvements to the economy. He obtained investments from other countries and he expanded the railways, trying to develop settlements in remote parts of Russia. Unfortunately, he was not favoured by Nicholas II but he began a process of economic advance and modernisation that continued to 1914.

Stolypin also promoted economic change and he supported the Duma. However, ministers such as Witte and Stolypin were seen as threats by the reactionary courtiers and the tsar usually listened to bad rather than good advice. Russia did have many problems in 1914, most of them centring on the tsar and his entourage but Russia was not 'terminally ill'.

Examiner's tip   The answer is developing well. The condition of Russia in 1914 is analysed convincingly and the candidate has taken the opportunity to use the quotations. The previous paragraph is a useful summary of the argument so far.

Nicholas II had managed to retain autocratic government over Russia in peacetime but the war caused him to lose control. The inefficiency of the army was exposed in heavy defeats against the German army. Soldiers lacked weapons and adequate clothing. They used methods of fighting which were disastrous against the well-armed Germans. The situation did not improve when the tsar took personal control and he was now blamed personally for failure.

The war effort and disruption to communications caused hardship at home. Famine spread and morale fell as soldiers returned home with their stories of defeat and incompetence. Three million Russian soldiers were probably killed, more than the combined casualties of Britain and France. Criticism spread from blame of the tsar to condemnation of his entire system of government. The tsarina, Alexandra, was a German and, although she had tried to make herself very Russian, she was suspected of being a traitor and it was known that she had great influence over Nicholas. Soldiers mutinied and civilians rioted in the streets. Traditionally, tsars had been able to use the army to crush disturbances while the secret police had dealt with political opponents. Neither of these could now be relied on. The army's loyalty evaporated while unrest was too widespread for the police to deal with.

In the face of all this opposition, and with his supporters discredited, Nicholas II abdicated. The war was to cause not only his abdication but the complete downfall of his system of government. The new government which followed the February Revolution continued the war but when Lenin and the Bolsheviks gained power in October, they promised peace. The whole country was war weary. The situation was so desperate that they agreed to make massive concessions to Germany in the Treaty of Brest-Litovsk (1918).

The war had killed the tsarist system and the republican Bolsheviks proceeded to kill the tsar and his family. In 1914 it seemed that the government of Nicholas II would probably survive, at least in the middle term. The war imposed insupportable strains on the system and brought unexpected opportunities to its enemies.

Examiner's tip The second half of the above answer deals with the other quotation. All of the points are relevant and they explain why tsarism fell. The essay is organised and well balanced. The style is clear. The brief conclusion is effective, summarising the main argument.

Question 2

Examiner's tip The key word is 'terror'. The question allows for other aspects of policy to be discussed ('a sufficient explanation') but, even if you disagree with the suggested explanation, it must be dealt with first.

Stalin's rule of terror extended into every corner of the USSR. Political enemies and rivals, social classes, army officers and members of racial minorities in the republics around Russia were exposed to widespread persecution. As more evidence emerges, historians agree that the extent of the terror and purges was greater than was previously thought.

The Bolsheviks had established a one-party state after the 1917 Revolution and Lenin imposed his will by force on his enemies. The tsar and his family were executed while his supporters were dealt with by the Cheka. However, this was not essentially different in intention and extent from the policies of Nicholas II and his predecessors in pre-revolutionary Russia. Nevertheless, Stalin used terror and suppression in a way that was different not only in scale but also in purpose.

Examiner's tip These two paragraphs introduce briefly the main lines of the argument and refer to previous developments. They do not waste time on less relevant background.

From 1929, the policy of agricultural collectivisation resulted in the destruction of the kulak class. They were deprived of their farms, deported or killed. The resulting famine, caused by the death of animals and falling harvests, was ignored because Stalin put a higher priority on achieving his aims of transforming the Soviet society and economy. He was also determined to industrialise the USSR. This involved the conscription of people to work in factories and the use of terror, as well as inducements, to punish anybody who did not meet production targets. Factory labourers, engineers and managers were accused of sabotage when quotas were not fulfilled. Stalin achieved his aims because production increased. However, he again ignored the fact that the gains were achieved only because of the hardship caused to millions and historians now even question whether the gains were as great as previously imagined because industry remained fundamentally inefficient. Stalin had shown his pre-eminence over the economy but at a very high cost to the Soviet population.

Terror was used to destroy political opposition and therefore enhance Stalin's personal position. He was ruthless and unscrupulous in defeating Trotsky after Lenin's death. Trotsky was stripped of his offices and then driven into exile. Even there he was not safe, being murdered by Stalinist agents in 1940. The terror was then extended to anyone who was suspected of Trotskyist sympathies.

In the 1930s, political terror resulted in a series of high-profile trials. From 1935 to 1938, eminent politicians and party members who had links with the 1917 Revolution and Lenin were charged with treason, usually alleging pro-German sympathies. Zinoviev and Kamenev were two of the leading 'Old Bolsheviks' who were executed. Stalin then moved against army generals and, having destroyed those at the top of the party and army, he proceeded against the middle and lower ranks. Thousands of party members and military officers were purged. As in the economic purges, the costs to human life and efficiency were ignored when Stalin's personal interests and policies were at stake. His motives are unclear. While it may be that he acted simply out of malice, historians now believe it possible that he perceived a real threat from elements in the USSR who would not cooperate, making him determined to remove completely groups that were not absolutely reliable. It is certainly true that people were purged because they belonged to specific groups rather than because of their individual actions. It is also undeniable that the result was that Stalin's pre-eminence was greater than ever.

> **Examiner's tip** At this point, the answer introduces other ideas. It has assessed successfully the importance of terror. It now develops alternative arguments. This shows a well-organised argument. The other points are presented relevantly.

However, although terror was important, it was not the only means by which Stalin gained so much power. He had become a member of the Politburo in 1919 and, from 1923, was in charge of party organisation. This gave him control over party officials and appointments which strengthened him in the power struggle against Trotsky. Unlike Hitler, who combined the offices of Chancellor, President and Commander-in-Chief, Stalin's formal position rested on his office as General Secretary. Not until 1941 did he become Prime Minister.

Rather than relying on the formality of offices, Stalin's pre-eminence was highly personal. Propaganda images portrayed him as almost above party or group, the father of the nation who was dedicated to the care of the population. People were convinced to such an extent that treason trials could be held in public and the accused confessed to crimes of which they were innocent. There is little evidence that the population associated Stalin with the hardships which they had to endure.

This fatherly image was underlined by propaganda, including the use of films which compared Stalin indirectly but clearly to the heroes of Russian history such as Peter the Great and even Ivan the Terrible. They portrayed the events of 1917 in a way that exaggerated the role of Stalin; agricultural and industrial scenes recorded only the happiness and success of workers, who all praised Stalin for their achievements.

With his rivals removed and the opposition crushed ruthlessly, Stalin could direct policy without risk of opposition. Unlike Hitler, who continued to be surrounded by quarrelling factions which pursued contradictory policies, Stalin had associates who did not dare to pursue their own lines; they carried out his wishes unhesitatingly. Historians now know that, although they enjoyed a privileged life-style, these associates, including important ministers, were often personally humiliated by Stalin.

Taken at face value, the purges of kulaks, party members and the military would seem to indicate that Stalin did face opposition but the reality is that they never threatened his pre-eminence and their destruction through terror was a means of enforcing and displaying publicly his power, which remained unthreatened during this period.

> **Examiner's tip** This essay is well focused. Always relevant, it considers alternative possibilities, examining first terror and then weighing it against other aspects. Factual knowledge is always related to the arguments.

Question 3

An answer which is heavily weighted to the downfall of tsarism will not be worth a high mark. Give equal attention to 1905 and 1917.

Examiner's answer plan

An introduction might include a short explanation of what happened in both revolutions. Then analyse and compare. In 1905 unrest was confined to a few places, e.g. St Petersburg; 1917 saw greater disturbances. In 1905, but not 1917, the tsar could rely on the army. The 1914 war had more serious effects than the Russo-Japanese War. When explaining 1917, your essay should show an awareness of both revolutions. The February Revolution did not destroy the tsarist system as did the October Revolution. Any discussion of the period between 1905 and 1914 must be related to the 1917 Revolution.

Question 4

This can be written as a two-part answer. Each part does not need to be of similar length but you must give equal attention to tsarist and Bolshevik rule. Note specified dates, especially 1929.

Examiner's answer plan

Similarities include use of (secret) police to suppress opposition, extreme dissent was suppressed; Russia still largely agricultural. Differences include republic had succeeded monarchy; Bolshevism had replaced tsarism; even moderate political parties were banned in 1929. A good conclusion would indicate which were the stronger, the similarities or differences. Avoid a continuous survey but concentrate on particular aspects.

Question 5

A structured essay. The length of each sub-answer should be guided by the mark allocation and by the specific instructions in the question. Be exact in your answers.

Examiner's answer plan

(a) 'Identify' does not mean explain; brief mentions only are needed, e.g. Bolsheviks, Social Democrats, tsarist.

(b) Give equal attention to war and land reform. Bolsheviks promised to end an unpopular war and to redistribute land.

(c) Bolshevik policies were popular because they met the main demands of the Russians: peace, food and liberty. However, only a minority were active supporters of the party.

(d) Avoid a narrative of the war but assess causes of Bolshevik victory, e.g. role of Trotsky and Red Army, divisions among Whites, lack of effective foreign aid.

Question 6

| **Examiner's tip** | A two-part question. A very good mark needs equal balance. Avoid approaching this question as a narrative of economic policies. |

Examiner's answer plan

An introduction should describe the New Economic Policy. Explain the combination of state control and some private enterprise. 'Why?' asks for reasons. Consider alternatives, e.g. Stalin saw Policy as politically unacceptable. Then assess the success of Stalin's policies. How far did they achieve their objectives, economic and political? A conclusion might be overall comparison of economy in 1917 and 1941.

12 NAZISM IN GERMANY, 1919–39

Question 1

| **Examiner's tip** | The key phrases are 'weakness of the Weimar Republic' and 'strength of the Nazi movement'. It is important to signify from the beginning which claim is stronger. Note that the question includes a specific end date. Answers should not go beyond 1933. |

Unlike Lenin and the Bolsheviks who triumphed in Russia after a revolution, Hitler and the Nazis gained power legally. In a way, Hitler did not seize power; it was given to him by the politicians of a weak Weimar Germany. Once in power, Hitler then used legal methods to impose a dictatorship. Although the Weimar Republic contributed much to its own downfall, it must be explained why, after establishing a fragile stability during the previous 15 years, it did not survive the rise of the Nazis.

| **Examiner's tip** | A good first sentence in which the comparison with Russia is brief. A longer comparison would have been less effective. The introduction shows which line of argument will be followed. |

Only four years before Hitler was appointed Chancellor (1933), the Weimar Republic seemed to be secure. Stresemann, the Foreign Secretary, had done much to restore Germany's fortunes. After the First World War, Germany had been heavily punished in the Treaty of Versailles, the War Guilt clause branded the Germans as criminals and the loss of colonies and reparations did immense damage to the economy. It was isolated from the League of Nations, and France, in particular, was determined to keep Germany weak. During his period of office from 1923, Stresemann took Germany into the League of Nations with a permanent seat on the Council which reflected Germany's acceptance as an important and respected country. The Locarno Pact helped to ease relations with Britain and France. The Dawes Plan (1924) modified the reparations, which helped Germany to recover from the intense inflation of the 1920s when unemployment had grown alarmingly and people's savings had disappeared. The employment situation improved and foreign investors were sufficiently confident to put their money into the German economy.

The Weimar Republic seemed to be pulling out of the problems of the 1920s when extreme left- and right-wing groups had used violence in attempts to seize power. The communist Spartacist rising of 1919 and the right-wing putsches of Kapp and Hitler at Munich were examples of the way in which extremists had been willing and able to cause trouble. Such threats seemed to recede during the more stable governments of the later 1920s but the improvement was fragile. Under the surface, there were still dangers which could reappear if the government's problems grew.

The constitution of the Republic made it difficult to sustain stable government. Many small parties were represented in the Reichstag because of proportional representation. Coalitions were usually short lived and some of the parties were more concerned about regional than about national issues.

The situation suddenly worsened in 1929 when Stresemann died and the Wall Street Crash affected every European economy, but especially Germany's. Conditions quickly deteriorated to resemble those of the early post-war years. However, while Weimar had survived the earlier crises, it now failed to cope. The main problem was that leading figures in the Republic were not loyal to Weimar. Hindenburg was elected President because of his military reputation not because of his political abilities. Von Papen challenged law and order in another putsch and he was not discredited; in fact he was to become Hitler's Vice-Chancellor. Industrialists and generals were more afraid of the communist threat than they were of right-wing extremists and they underestimated Hitler. Although they were not Nazis, they sympathised with much of the Nazi programme, such as extreme nationalism, revision of Versailles and anti-semitism.

| **Examiner's tip** | The answer has dealt successfully with the weakness of Weimar. It avoids a narrative of events from 1918 but considers their significance. The focus is on the situation in 1929. |

Hitler led the Nazis from insignificance, one of many small groups, to become a major party and he benefited as voters abandoned moderate policies and favoured extreme measures. In 1930 the Nazis won slightly more seats in the Reichstag than the communists and by 1932 they were well ahead. A slight drop in the vote in a second election did little to change the impression that the Nazis were a rising force with a membership of a million. The leaders of Weimar were in a quandary because no other group could establish an effective and lasting government. Hindenburg and the others believed that Hitler would become a respectable political leader once he was given power and that the Nazis were less of a risk than the communists.

Hitler was a very effective party leader. A powerful orator, he promised to solve all of Germany's problems, especially the Jews who were held primarily responsible for the country's difficulties. Anti-semitism was widespread in Germany and other parts of Europe and the Nazis' attacks on the Jews proved to be popular in winning votes. Propaganda glorified Hitler and enabled him to spread his ideas in simple and effective ways. Meanwhile the SA threatened opponents and bullied people into supporting the party.

When other politicians were scrambling for power in the coalitions, Hitler refused to join unless the Nazis were given a dominant position and those in the party who favoured joining coalitions were expelled. His gamble paid off. Hindenburg and the other politicians felt that there was no alternative but to appoint Hitler as Chancellor. Of course, they were persuaded by the strength of the Nazi Party but it was weakness which drove their policy and this weakness then led to the acceptance and approval of his measures as Chancellor. Politicians had used emergency powers before 1933 and the Enabling Act, which suspended the constitution, was only a more extreme example of what had been done previously.

Nazi propaganda was successful in persuading people of the threat from communism. The Roman Catholic Church changed its critical tone and gave approval to Hitler's measures. Other political parties were banned, the SA terrorised rivals and the Nazis took control of the police. Within a year of gaining power legally, Hitler had also established a dictatorship – again legally. He had done so through the strength of his personality and the wide support for Nazi ideas but fundamentally he succeeded because of the weakness and miscalculations of the leaders of the Weimar Republic.

> **Examiner's tip** The answer will score highly because of relevance, analysis and clarity of argument. Knowledge is accurate and sufficiently detailed. The answer avoids vagueness and is very thoughtful. The answer is successful in dealing with both Weimar and the Nazis.

Question 2

> **Examiner's tip** The extract is included as stimulus material, intended to help you to shape your ideas. You will very probably agree that it is true. The questions do not require you to use it during an answer.

(a) By the mid-1930s, Hitler's regime seemed to represent everything for which Germany hoped and it had not fully revealed those repressive aspects which might cause it to be unpopular. From 1929, it seemed as if the Weimar Republic might return to the conditions which had caused economic distress and social divisions during the 1920s. Following the Wall Street Crash, the withdrawal of American investments had resulted in serious economic dislocation. People still remembered the times when their savings had been wiped out and their wages had been worthless because of rampant inflation during the 1920s. Unemployment spread and there was a fear of a communist-style revolution.

The Nazis had emerged in the 1920s as an extreme group which used violence to achieve its aims and Hitler had carried out an unsuccessful putsch in Munich in 1923. The Nazis had not abandoned these methods but Hitler had also made the Nazis into a mass party by careful organisation and by appealing to the widespread feelings in Germany. By 1930, the Nazis were the second largest political party in Germany. To right-wing groups of industrialists and army generals, they were preferable to left-wing communists.

Hitler claimed that he would reverse the losses at the Treaty of Versailles and that he would take revenge on the 'November criminals' who had betrayed Germany and its soldiers. His anti-semitic teaching enjoyed much support in a country which blamed the Jews for all of its troubles. The Weimar politicians proved ineffective and therefore Hitler's defence of a strong ruler, or Führer, was attractive especially as it was not clear that he would destroy democracy once he had gained power. When he became Chancellor in 1933 he enjoyed support from most sections of the population. The wealthy saw him as a defender of capitalism against revolution, the poor saw in the Nazis their best chance of prosperity. All were united in supporting his determination to make Germany great again and to punish those who had harmed its interests.

He gained power using the legal machinery of the Weimer Republic and, although he quickly increased his authority after the Reichstag fire, introducing the Enabling Laws, the full implication of this was not seen by the mid-1930s. Public works, anti-Jewish measures and the propaganda of Goebbels enabled Hitler to appear as the true champion of the Germans. His early moves to strengthen the German army and his acceptance by foreign governments added to his popularity.

> **Examiner's tip** The above section is worthwhile because it analyses and explains the different aspects of Hitler's popularity. The question does not ask for an assessment of his unpopularity and therefore the question is addressed directly.

(b) The Nazis were determined to suppress all opposition to, or even any deviation from, their policies. The SA, under Rohm, were not enemies. These Brownshirts had been used to terrorise opponents in street fighting but their image was now unpopular with the wealthy and influential people who had agreed to give power to Hitler and he assassinated the leaders of the SA in the Night of the Long Knives in 1934. However, this did not mark the end of violence by the Nazis. Having reassured those who hated the SA, Hitler used the SS and Gestapo to enforce his policies. These were more organised and disciplined. The SS tried to recruit the sons of well-to-do people in an effort to persuade people of its respectability while it also persecuted mercilessly the enemies of the regime.

When Hindenburg died in 1934, Hitler became President and Commander-in-Chief, thus gaining authority over the armed forces. All soldiers swore obedience to the Führer and opposition was not significant, even during the last days of the war. At least one assassination plot was attempted but it had little support from the military. Certainly during the 1930s Hitler exerted control over the military.

Other political parties were banned. Politicians who had been active in Weimar and who showed any signs of resistance to the new government were arrested. Communists were also a prime target. State officials, down to the least important, had to be members of the Nazi Party. This policy included judges and civil servants while teachers were pressurised to become party members. Trade unions were replaced by the government-controlled Labour Front.

The Nazis attacked particular social groups, the most important of which were the Jews. Boycotts of Jewish shops and businesses were replaced by legislation which prevented marriages between 'Aryan' German and Jews and in 1935 the Nuremberg Laws, produced during the fervent rallies in which Hitler whipped up frenzied support, deprived Jews of their civil rights. The pressure continued to increase until ultimately the Jews were sent to concentration camps for extermination. The Jews did not represent any threat to Hitler but they were seen as enemies whose extermination represented control. Such control was extended to other unpopular groups which deviated from Aryan ideals, such as gypsies and homosexuals.

Propaganda was an important means of exerting control. As Minister of Enlightenment and Propaganda, Goebbels governed the ways in which the Germans saw Hitler and the Nazis. Rallies, marches, posters focused on Hitler as the leader. In the cinema, films portrayed German ideals and anti-semitic propaganda. Styles in art, architecture and sculpture were expected to reflect German strength and avoid what was regarded as decadent. The lives of children were directed through state organisations while schools taught a Nazi curriculum. Sport was used as a means of control when Nazi methods were seen as most successful, culminating in the displays of the 1936 Olympics.

Control was therefore exerted directly and indirectly. On the one hand, the regime used terror and repression while, on the other, it used the methods of propaganda. The control was used effectively. There was no significant opposition to Hitler by 1939 and he even managed to persuade many people in other countries that his policies and methods were justified. Indeed, it was only defeat in war in 1945 and not a rising of Germans that brought about the ultimate fall of the Nazi regime.

Examiner's tip The answer gets credit for its emphasis on 'control'. It avoids description but concentrates on 'How effectively'. The conclusion is a brief but worthwhile summary of the argument.

Question 3

Examiner's tip This question depends on clear understanding of Versailles. In particular (a) and (b) depend on specific knowledge. Use the mark allocation to guide the length of your answers.

Examiner's answer plan

(a) States 'identify', not explain. Include four different points, e.g. territory, War Guilt Clause, loss of armaments, reparations.

(b) Avoid general statements but base answer on point made in (a).

(c) 'To what extent' allows for other factors but deal first with Versailles as a cause of Hitler's rise, e.g. extreme nationalism, 'stab in the back'.

(d) Note key dates, 1933–9. You can disagree, but first explain anti-Versailles feeling.

Question 4

Examiner's tip Before writing decide which quotation is more valid. Then discuss this first before considering the alternative.

Examiner's answer plan

- The introduction should clarify your argument.
- 'Noble experiment': very democratic; toleration of minority groups.
- 'Positive achievements': Weimar survived the problems of early 1920s; economy improved; better relations with other countries; largely overcame War Guilt.
- 'Hated ... powerful group': association with 1918 defeat and Versailles; right-wing politicians, business men, etc disliked it; no firm backing for democracy; extremists used violence.
- Avoid a chronological survey of 1918–33.

Letts
Q&A

Question 5

Examiner's tip The key words are 'by 1938' and 'inherited from the Weimar Republic'. Descriptions of Nazi policy will be relevant only if they are linked to the period before 1933.

Examiner's answer plan
First explain the internal problems of Weimar in 1932 avoiding a general narrative of Weimar since 1919. Discuss political instability, unstable coalitions, lack of firm leadership. Economic problems include inflation, unemployment, loss of resources in Saar and overseas. Explain 'by 1938', that is before war. Do not write a general survey of Hitler's Germany. A conclusion should include an overall assessment, weighing the successes and failures.

Question 6

Examiner's tip The key words are 'purely "opportunist"'. A very good answer will consider the case for and against the claim, showing why one is preferable.

Examiner's answer plan
State your overall case clearly in your introduction. Then consider the alternatives, e.g. if you disagree and believe that he planned events, explain how far he relied on the actions and policies of others. The question does not mention specific years but do not write a survey. Concentrate on important events, e.g. seizure of Czechoslovakia, invasion of Poland, attack on USSR. How far did he pursue his initial aims and how far did he change?

13 SOURCE-BASED QUESTIONS

Question 1
(a) (i) Indirect taxes or taxes on food, e.g. corn.
(ii) People available for work.
(iii) Work provided by government, e.g. road building.
(b) Document I advocates lowering indirect taxes so that the cost of basic foods will be reduced. This will also leave more money to be spent on manufactured goods. The other strategies proposed are directed towards reducing the excess labour supply, which the author blames for low wages. He proposes state assistance to enable children to be sent to school and women to stay at home. He urges the government to encourage emigration, which will also reduce the labour supply. Finally, employment can be created by public works.
(c) The tone of Document II is polite. The petitioners are careful to refer to the House of Commons as 'your Honourable House'. Nevertheless their views are forcefully expressed: wages are described not as low but as 'inadequate' and working hours are 'protracted beyond the limits of endurance'. The language is colourful – 'wretched and unparalleled' – and, despite the deferential tone, the petitioners' criticism of the government is uncompromising: they accuse it of doing nothing to reduce inequality between rich and poor or to 'promote general prosperity'.

(d) Macaulay's main point is that the government cannot do what the Chartists want. The date of his speech shows that he is referring to Chartist demands for government support for the people – demands such as those set out in Documents I and II. Document I proposes public assistance for those on low wages and public works to create employment while Duncombe in Document II demands lower taxation to increase prosperity and reduced working hours. Macaulay argues that the government does not have the resources to do these things. Underlying his argument are his laissez-faire views. He would not see it as the government's function to interfere in the economy and attempt to increase wages or reduce working hours.

(e) Document I refers to a number of grievances: taxes on food, unemployment, low wages and the employment of children. Document II also refers to low wages, along with excessive hours of work. It describes the condition of the people graphically as 'wretched and unparalleled' and protests against the inequality between rich and poor, an idea which can also be found in the opening lines of Document I ('the many and the few'). Both documents accuse Parliament of failing to do anything about the condition of the people. Both are direct evidence of Chartist grievances, Document I being taken from a Chartist newspaper in 1839 and Document II from the 1842 Chartist petition. The late 1830s and early 1840s were a period of economic depression which did produce unemployment and low wages, as described in these documents, and much of the support for Chartism at this time was the result of hardship. There were, however, other reasons. The Charter itself had its origin in working-class disappointment at exclusion from the vote by the 1832 Reform Act. There was much working-class hostility to the Poor Law Amendment Act with its workhouse 'Bastilles'. The collapse of the Grand National Trade Union led some of the working class to turn to Chartism. Chartism gained some of its impetus from the support of middle-class radicals like Attwood, while O'Connor was important in whipping up support. Finally Chartism was in many ways a collection of local movements; much of its support derived from local grievances.

Question 2

> **Examiner's tip** There are 3 marks for each part of (a), so the Examiners are expecting more than a definition.

(a) (i) Under the Poor Law of 1834 the able-bodied poor were taken into the workhouse, but old people who were no longer able to work could receive outdoor relief. This meant that they were given money payments to support themselves. In the context of Extract B, this reference shows that many old people had previously had to rely on the Poor Law.

(ii) The National Insurance scheme set up in 1911 provided (a) insurance against sickness for most of the working class, financed by contributions from the employee, the employer and the state; (b) insurance against unemployment for workers in certain industries. The scheme was the work of Lloyd George and this is why in Extract D he refers to it with such pride.

(b) Extract B – by a historian – shows pensions reduced poverty by relieving most of the aged poor of the need to rely on the Poor Law. They 'served a major social need' (figures are quoted to support this) and were very popular. Lloyd George was generally given the credit; indeed, the elderly poor believed he must be a 'lord'. Extract D (Lloyd George's own words) describes National Insurance as intended to 'drive away privation and hunger' and in the last paragraph presents a vision of a country from which poverty has been banished. His words have a crusading ring about them.

(c) Extracts A and C set out some of the main points in two of the most important Liberal reforms, the Pensions and National Insurance Acts. These introduced state responsibility for helping people to cope with the financial problems of old age, sickness and unemployment. Extract B shows how successful the pension scheme was, while in Extract D Lloyd George describes the National Insurance scheme as 'mobilising the nation' in a crusade to improve health and 'drive away privation'. Clearly these two Acts represent a significant extension of state responsibility for the welfare of British citizens.

The Liberal governments also increased state responsibility in other ways not illustrated in the extracts. To improve the health of children, particularly the children of the poor, school meals and school medical inspections were introduced, and further protection was provided for vulnerable children by the 'Children's Charter'. To protect workers in the 'sweated industries', trade boards were set up, and conditions were improved for shop workers and miners by the Shops Act and the Mines Act. The unemployed were helped to find work by the establishment of labour exchanges.

Important though the reforms were (some would regard them as the foundation of the welfare state), there were limitations. The Poor Law was not reformed. Unemployment insurance was limited to the buildings and engineering trades. The old age pension was very small and it was provided only for the poorest old people. The National Insurance scheme was only a pointer towards modern ideas of social security – indeed, Wood describes it as 'no more than a refinement of the nineteenth-century doctrine of self-help – with the encouragement of a benevolent state'.

> **Examiner's tip** You will get no more than 6 marks out of 10 if you do not include material both from the extracts and from your own knowledge and also make some explicit judgement about 'how extensively' the Liberals increased state responsibility.

Question 3

> **Examiner's tip** As in all source-based questions, note the mark allocation and organise your time accordingly. Answer all the questions very precisely. Pay particular attention to whether you need to use the sources only or refer to your own knowledge of the topic.

(a) (i) Schacht was President of the Reichsbank and was regarded as Hitler's chief financial adviser.

(ii) Goebbels was in charge of Nazi propaganda and an important figure in the government. An intellectual, he was contemptuous about many other Nazis, especially those whom he felt to be uneducated.

(iii) The SS had been developed from the personal bodyguard of Hitler. They felt a mission to advance Nazism and regarded themselves as select.

(b) Führer power was not limited by the state or any public laws and was therefore superior to any other authority. It represented the general will of the German people and applied to every aspect of German life. In practice, this demanded obedience from every person who surrendered individual rights.

(c) Speer was an associate of Hitler who could write about Nazi government from the inside. This contributes to the reliability of the extract. However, the source was not written until 1970 and it might well be that Speer was writing with hindsight, trying to justify himself and distance himself from the worst excesses of Hitler's regime. Nevertheless, his description of factions is partly supported by the other extracts, e.g.

Documents C and D, which describe rivalries and confusion, and his descriptions of leaders such as Goebbels and Goering are reliable. Overall, he can be seen as convincing.

(d) Document C describes a government characterised by inefficiency but Dietrich claims that Hitler was deliberately using disorder to increase his own authority. Document A supports the view that Hitler was reluctant to make decisions, continually postponing matters. Although the evidence is not direct, there is no reason to think that the writer was not recording what he had heard. There is some agreement about Hitler's motives in that Document A claims that the Führer thought that delay was beneficial. Document D, written by somebody who observed Hitler at close-hand, describes a system in which decisions were not made in an efficient manner but depended on chance. To this extent, it agrees with Document C but there is no hint that Hitler was deliberate. Document E confirms Document C in more detail. Speer contrasts the public image of Hitler with the private situation in which rival groups could act separately. Although the four documents differ about the extent to which Hitler intended to bring about the situation, they are agreed about how his methods worked in practice.

(e) Document B is the only source which indicates that the Nazi state was centrally directed and efficient. However, in describing the office of Führer, Huber, a theorist, was describing the ideas behind the constitution rather than the practical situation. Document C sees Hitler as directing affairs although the way in which he did so was to destroy efficiency. The other sources describe in different ways a government which was inefficient and lacking in direction. Overall, they deny the propaganda image of the Nazi regime although this was hidden from the general public. Propaganda was careful to show Hitler as dominant. Rallies, such as those at Nuremberg, put Hitler in the limelight and surrounded him with vast crowds and elaborate ceremonies. Films and radio broadcasts portrayed him as the great leader. Officials swore allegiance to him personally. However, the regime was indeed efficient in destroying its enemies, members of other groups which the government opposed and particularly the Jews. The SS and Gestapo prosecuted any signs of dissent and people were arrested on the slightest grounds of suspicion. Although Hitler himself might not have fulfilled his propaganda image, he always directed ultimate policy and his regime was ruthlessly efficient in maintaining control.

Question 4

Examiner's answer plan

(i) Do not simply identify types of evidence, e.g. memorandum; conversation; diary. **'Comment'** means that you must assess their weight as types of evidence.

(ii) **Avoid summarising** the documents. Look for similarities, e.g. Charles Antony's reluctance. What do the extracts show us of his attitudes to Bismarck and Prussia? Is the evidence reliable? Note to whom he is writing.

(iii) **Focus** on the relationship between Bismarck and William I. The relationship was not one-sided. Consider the significance of the king's insertions in Document B. Up to 10 marks for use of the documents only but 'How far' allows you to use your own knowledge to assess the extracts, giving an additional 5 marks.

(iv) This is a question on the documents only – not own knowledge. Note the **key word** 'nationalism'. Answers which discuss German unification generally will not deserve a high mark. Explain how 'nationalism' is apparent in these documents, e.g. Document A, 'supreme consciousness of Prussia's political power'. Discuss relationship with monarchy.